President Droupadi Murmu

A Reflection of changing Bharat

President Droupadi Murmu

A Reflection of changing Bharat

DR. VIJAYA LAKSHMI MOHANTY

GYAN

ISBN: 978-81-212-6470-9

Published, 2023

Published by

Gyan Publishing House
5, Ansari Road
Daryaganj, New Delhi-110002
Phone: 011-47034999, 9811692060
www.gyanbooks.com
E-mail: books@gyanbooks.com

Printed at: Gyan Press, Delhi.

Contents

Preface

On 21 June 2022 evening, I was logging off from the online Faculty Development Programme organised by me as the Director, Human Resource Development Centre, Sri Sri University, and my father came rushing with a humongous piece of news. It was an International Day of Yoga, and I was in my hometown Rairangpur. In no time, I found myself in front of the television to see that our very own Droupadi Murmu had been nominated as the Presidential candidate of National Democratic Alliance (NDA). The whole household jumped with joy, and we soon came out of our home to share the news with everyone around. We then proceeded towards her home near our place. My father insisted on taking a bouquet and all the florists had closed by then. We had to reopen a florist's shop to make a bouquet and proceed towards her home nearby.

Droupadi didi's first reaction after seeing me was to ask me when I returned to my hometown Rairangpur from my workplace at Sri Sri University, Cuttack. On seeing my father, both got emotional, and tears of gratitude rolled out from their eyes which were captured as the first broadcast shot of the day. People started pouring in, and the day turned to night. However, Rairangpur town did not sleep that night. She soon moved to New Delhi and the process of her nomination, campaigning, election, swearing in etc followed. The media had gathered in her hometown, her birthplace, her in-laws' village and the residential school in that village. I accompanied many media personnel to curate her unique story. It was during this time, that many well-wishers of Droupadi Murmu expressed that they wanted an authentic biographical sketch to be written on her. Though I was quite fascinated with the idea,

Dr. Taradatt, IAS strengthened my commitment to take this idea to fruition.

However, writing a book on her was not an easy task. I had thought because of my being an acquaintance, it would not too difficult. But I discovered a huge part of her personality in the nine-month research that went into writing an authentic biographical sketch on the magnificent personality called Droupadi Murmu. My reverence for her increased manifold from the core of my heart, for the values she has internalised throughout her life despite all odds. She embraced challenges with an undying smile while serving people for the last three decades through teaching, participating in the socio-cultural life of tribals, and of course politics. It is also a sweet coincidence that she wrote a message for my first book, 'Human Values and Ethics in Education' released by Gurudev Sri Sri Ravi Shankar on my birthday, 1 September 2015. Since she is a bibliophile, I thought this would be the best gift I can give on her behalf to humanity.

We are often taught to be mighty, powerful, go-getters and acquire skills to win the world. This defines success. This book however teaches these values in a different manner. If you are focused to serve and bring smiles in your neighbourhood by volunteering goodness, you will be noticed and rewarded. Nature is the mightiest. If you give something to it, it gives you back a manifold.

I present to you the most unassuming and simple real-life story of contemporary times based on goodness, camaraderie, simplicity, service, resilience, endurance and above all the zest for life. I share a proud moment with my countrymen and feel privileged that I hail from the same domicile as Hon'ble President Droupadi Murmu. Writing a book on her was an extremely divine experience for me. I was vicariously undergoing the agony and ecstasy in my body and mind as I was penning down this real-life story. For example, while writing the most difficult chapter 8 (Tragedies and Triumphs)

I had conjunctivitis for three weeks. I also starved myself for a few days to understand how it feels to be hungry. It has been no less than a spiritual awakening for me.

May her story inspire millions to be on the righteous path. May her story enthuse many women to take up the challenges by being more valorous. May her career teach us ethical political leadership. Every societal issue that we discussed with her, we see actions taken on the same in some form or the other within a very short time. Some of the issues include conservation of Simlipal national park, campaign for an addiction free Bharat, conservation of water bodies in our hometown Rairangpur, creation of a separate Rairangpur district etc. During one of my meetings with the Hon'ble President of Bharat on 17 April 2023, she expressed her opinion that all the citizens must be aware of the preamble, fundamental rights and fundamental duties. I have pledged to propagate the same through a civil society awakening called 'Volunteer for Good.'

A lot more can be written about her. I have made a sincere effort to capture as many facets as I can to the best of my ability. I hope this story leaves you inspired to find the best in you.

Acknowledgement

With the Blessings of my Master Gurudev Sri Sri Ravi Shankar, founder of the Art of Living humanitarian organization, present globally in 180 countries and founder, Sri Sri University, Cuttack, Odisha, India, I have started writing the book. Revered Bhanumathi Narasimhan, sister of Gurudev Sri Sri Ravi Shankar and Chairperson of Women's Welfare and Child Care programmes of The Art of Living, world-renowned meditation teacher has given the much-needed motivation by sending blessings for the book, **President Droupadi Murmu- A reflection of changing Bharat.**

We live in an interdependent world. A big part of me owe to the following who have helped me in completion of the book: My parents Manoranjan (Nandia) Mohanty, Dr. P.S. Manikyeswari; Ranu, my beloved aunt Late Bichitra Mohanty, my beloved uncle Late Anil Kumar Mohanty, Late Gyana Ranjan Mohanty, Aman, Abhigyan, Srinivas, Sushil Kumar Mohanty, Jayashree, Meenakshi, Sandhya, Manas, Spandan, Sachetan, Meghna, Ujjwal, Nirmalya, P.Neelaveni, PKV Gouripati Sastry, PKV Sastry, Dinesh Parida, Rajesh Madaan, Anjana Madaan, Shreya Batra, Vaibhav Batra, Dr. Manoj Bajaj, Hemalata Mohanta, Mamata Mohanta, Bikash Mohanta, Ranjita Mohanta, Rasananda Lenka, my bigger family members of Rairangpur, Uparbeda, Pahadpur, New Delhi, President Droupadi Madam's teachers, friends, party workers, government officials who worked with her etc. More than 100 people close to her life have been interviewed and it took nearly nine months of hard work to come up with this well-researched true content.

Dr. Taradatt, IAS (Ret'd) had put the sankalpa to write the book on the topic and introduced me to the publishers Gyan books, B.P. Garg and Amit Garg. His Eminence Dr. Parmeswar Nath

Mishra has helped me in freezing a suitable title. I am immensely grateful to President Droupadi Murmu's teachers Bisweswar Mohanta, Basant Giri, Basudev Behera; her family Taranisen Tudu, Sakramani Tudu, Itishree Murmu, Ganesh Murmu, Dhani Marandi, Dularam Tudu, Dulari Tudu, Menaka Tudu, Braja Mohan Murmu, Sanjukta Majhi; official staff, Rajesh Verma, Sampada Suresh Mehta, Santosh Kumar Satpathy, Surat Kumar Mohanta; teachers and students of SLS Memorial Residential School, Pahadpur, Mayurbhanj etc.

I feel privileged to get an opportunity to be the founding member of Sri Sri University, Cuttack, Odisha. It is like my prodigy and the university family has showered huge support to write the biographical sketch. Let me name a few out of hundreds of well-wishers, Prof. B.R.Sharma, Kusum Sharma, Prof. Ajay Kumar Singh, Sonali Das, Bharat Dash, Sthirata Dei, Dr. Malay Malla, Prof. Kalyani Samantray, Prof. Kamala Prasad Mohapatra, Mayank Madaan, Kapil Rajwani, Ashutosh Mohapatra, Krishna Ashrit Patnaik, Ram Vyas, Abhishek Ghose, Chaitanya Ram Dumbhare, Aayush Kapoor, Vishal Dewan, Rohit Sharma, Priyamwada Chettri, Arpit Srivastava, Smriti Chourasia, Siddhartha Pachourey, Adarsh Singh, Piyush Raj, Vridhi Mishra, Aarnav Adhikari, Niyati Mishra; her friends, Delha Soren, Dangi Murmu, Tapati Mandal, Chinmayee Gacchayat, Suchitra Samal, Prof. Archita Patnaik; her former teacher colleagues, Indira Otta, Kalpana Mohanty and students; her political proteges, Late Rabindra Nath Mohanta, Navin Kumar Ram, Naba Charan Majhi, Satish Chandra Pratihari, Shiv Shankar Agrawal, Manoj Das, Sanjib Mohanty, Sunil Mohanta, Dushmanta Basa, Niraj Panda, Purna Chandra Mohanta, Shashank Kumar and many more. The eminent authors, Swapnalekha Basak and Deepa Bhalerao did necessary edits. I can acknowledge till eternity and still there may be someone I have not thanked enough. I apologise! Thank you for sharing the dream of bringing this book which talks about a pure soul, walked ever on this planet, a reality.

I thank Almighty for all the moments spent with Honourable President Smt. Droupadi Murmu in the last three decades and the precious time spent in Rashtrapati Bhawan to complete the book. My life is also enriched by her unconditional love and affection towards me and my family.

List of Colour Illustrations

Droupadi with mother Singo & brother Taranisen

Droupadi Murmu With late husband Shyam Charan Murmu

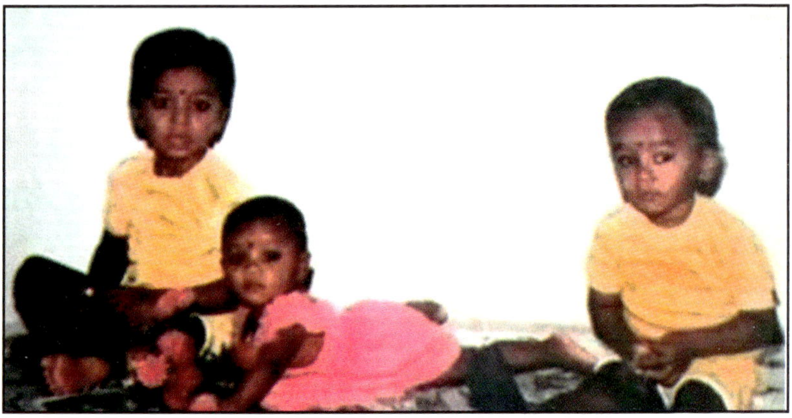

Droupadi's three children Laxman, Sipun & Itishree

Two sons, Late Laxman Murmu (Lucky) &
Late Biranchi Narayan Murmu (Sipun)

Inauguration of life size statue of Guru Gomke Pandit Raghunath Murmu donated by Droupadi Murmu, MLA, Raiarngpur placed in the Jaher Garh at Bhubaneswar in presence of Naveen Patnaik, Chief Minister on 11.01.2009

Inauguration in Kukudimundi, by Droupadi Murmu, Minister Department of Fisheries and Animal Resources Development, Government of Odisha in 2002

Walking her way in the Chadipahadi jungle along with constituents of Raiarngpur Assembly Constituency

Re-Construction of 'Sri Khadakeswar Shiva Temple' From MLALAD, established by late Sri Gopal Chandra Ram

Distribution camp of aids and appliances to special children by Droupadi Murmu, MLA, Raiarngpur, V.K.Pandian,District Collector, Mayurbhanj, Satya Kumar Mallick, Sub-Collector, Raiarangpur at Dubulabeda Primary School, Rairangpur on 15.10.2005

Inauguration of classroom at Badamtalia High school 14.11.2005

Mahamahim Droupadi Murmu Swearing in as the Governor of Jharkhand on 18.05.2015 in Ranchi

Mahamahim Droupadi Murmu accompanied by Raghubar Das, Chief Minister of Jharkhand after the Swearing in as the Governor of Jharkhand on 18.05.2015

Hon'ble Governor Droupadi Murmu, receiving Gurudev Sri Sri Ravi Shankar in Raj Bhawan, Ranchi on 04.03.2017

Worshiping Lord Jagannath, Lord Balabhadra and Goddess Subhadra during Rath Yatra at Rairangpur

Met Pranab Mukherjee, President of India during her period as the Governor of Jharkhand

Inauguration in Kukudimundi, by Droupadi Murmu, Minister Department of Fisheries and Animal Resources Development, Government of Odisha in 2002

Swearing in of Hemant Soren, Chief Minister of Jharkhand by Mahamahim Droupadi Murmu on 29.12.2019

Rath Yatra celebration at Rairangpur during her period as Governor, Jharkhand in 2016

Felicitating meritorious students under the aegis of SLS Trust Board in Rairangpur as the Governor of Jharkhand

Students and teachers of SLS Memorial Residential School,Odisha, August 2022

Droupadi Murmu received by Narendra Modi, Prime Minister, India at New Delhi in June 2022

Droupadi Murmu is received by Amit Shah, Minister of Home Affairs of Bharat in June 2022

Naveen Patnaik, Chief Minister, Odisha receives NDA Presidential candidate Droupadi Murmu in Odisha Legislative Assembly on 08.07.2022

Family dinner hosted by outgoing President Ram Nath Kovind for the president-elect Droupadi Murmu in July 2022

Mahamahim Droupadi Murmu, the newly appointed 15th President of Bharat administered oath of ethics by N.V. Ramana, Chief Justice of Bharat on 25.07.2022

Dinner hosted by outgoing President Ram Nath Kovind for Mahamahim Droupadi Murmu, the newly appointed 15th President of India in July 2022

The ceremonial picture of outgoing President Ram Nath Kovind and the new President Droupadi Murmu at Rastrapati Bhawan, Raisina Hills, New Delhi on 25.07.2023

Swearing in ceremony of President Droupadi Murmu at Central Hall of Parliament, New Delhi on 25 July 2022

Tri-Services Guard of Honour for President Droupadi Murmu in Rastrapati Bhawan, New Delhi on 25.07.2022

Author of the book Dr. Vijaya Lakshmi Mohanty meeting Honourable President Droupadi Murmu on 28.08.2022 at Rastrapati Bhawan, New Delhi

Mahamahim Droupdi Murmu, Governor of Jharkhand attending Social Programme in Rairangpur

Honourable President Droupadi Murmu Manoranjan (Nandia) Mohanty, Dr. P.S. Manikyeswari, Aman Mohanty, family of the author, Dr. Vijaya Lakshmi Mohanty on 04.05.2023 in Rairangpur

Chapter - 1

Destiny's Daughter (1958 - 1963)

The story unfolds in Uparbeda.

If you are thinking, it is a place which you may fail to find in the Global Positioning System, situated somewhere at the end of the world, you can't be more wrong! The political contribution of this high-octane village may well be considered as the 'cradle of tribal politics of not only the state but the country too'. Uparbeda a village on the banks of the Kanhu River is in the Kusumi Block, Bamanghaty (Rairangpur) Sub-Division of Mayurbhanj district of Odisha. It is approximately 280 kilometres from the state capital, Bhubaneswar and 14 kilometres from Rairangpur municipality. Even though many parts of the Mayurbhanj district have fertile land, due to the presence of mountains and rivers, the density of population is lesser than that of the coastal districts of Odisha. Mayur-bhanj comprises four subdivisions namely Baripada, Bamanghaty/ Rairangpur, Panchpid/ Karanjia and Kaptipada/Udala. Bamanghaty was called Brahmanaghaty and Panchpid was called Pancha Peedha in the nineteenth century. Mayurbhanj district has four Urban Local Bodies (hereafter referred to as ULBs), two Municipalities namely Baripada, Rairangpur and two Notified Area Councils (hereafter, NACs) namely Karanjia and Udala. It has 3966 villages, 404 Gram Panchayats, 26 tehsils, 26 blocks, and 32 police stations. With an area of 10,418 square kilometres, Mayurbhanj is the largest district among the thirty districts of Odisha in eastern India. In terms of population, it is the third most populous district after Ganjam and Cuttack, having a total population of 2,519,738 out of which 1,479,576 are tribals (census, 2011). Baripada is the district headquarters of Mayurbhanj district, while Rairangpur is the headquarters of Bamanghaty sub-division.

The Santhals comprise one of the dominant tribes among the sixty-two scheduled tribes in the state of Odisha. They live predominantly in the Mayurbhanj, Keonjhar and Sundergarh districts of the state as also in Singhbhum district of Jharkhand and Birbhum district of West Bengal among others. Central India witnesses the presence of tribals even though Bharat registers approximately 705 numbers of tribes comprising approximately nine percent of its total population. Tribal politics has always been a focal point in the country's politics. For many centuries, successive rulers tried to do welfare, woo, divide and rule the community for the sake of gaining their support for the ease of administration. The governance story of the last two centuries of the tribal dominated Mayurbhanj has also been equally interesting.

Though the land of Mayurbhanj has produced great leaders for generations, the post-independence story of the democratic polity started with Karthik Chandra Majhi, son of Chandra Mohan Majhi, a lawyer by profession. He contested the election from Rairangpur constituency and was elected in 1967 with the Swatantra Party ticket. He became the finance minister of the state under the Chief Ministership of Rajendra Narayan Singhdeo. As a cabinet minister, Majhi also held the portfolios of Home, Urban Development, Works, Transport from 1967-71. He happens to be a relative of Droupadi Murmu, the 15th President of India.

Bhabendra Nath Majhi followed the tradition to contest elections in 1985 on the ticket of Indian National Congress (hereafter, INC) and won from the same constituency. A mining engineer by profession, he was MLA for just a year, as he passed away on 31 March 1986.

Droupadi Murmu, the first lady legislator from the same constituency, was elected for two consecutive times for the 12th Assembly (2000-2004) and 13th Assembly (2004-2009) elections. She was the Minister of State, Commerce and Transport from March 2000 to August 2002, and Minister of State, Fisheries and Animal Resources Development from August 2002 to May 2004, with independent charge both the time. Statistically, out of 13 legislators that Rairangpur Constituency has elected in 16 elections and 1 by-election, three hail from Uparbeda. The story does not end here.

Salkhan Murmu, another political leader with ancestry from Uparbeda won the election in 1998 and in 1999 as a Member of Parliament from Mayurbhanj Parliamentary Constituency as a Bharatiya Janata Party (hereafter, BJP) candidate. However, Uparbeda witnessed the zenith of political activity with the elevation of Droupadi Murmu as the Governor of Jharkhand, and, subsequently, as the President of Bharat.

The pre-independence history of Uparbeda, Rairangpur, Bamanghaty, Mayurbhanj is glorious as well as breath-taking, replete with a galaxy of dynamic tribal leaders. An overview of this history will throw light on the origin of the lineage of the Sardar family, to which Droupadi Murmu belongs. Who is a Sardar? What are his/her powers? What was the hierarchy of governance like during that time? It is impossible to know the legacy of Sardars without knowing the history of two centuries of Rairangpur and Mayurbhanj. Even the contemporary generation living in Mayurbhanj is not familiar with this history.

The Bhanja and the Bhujanga dynasties ruled Mayurbhanj. In the year 1835, Mayurbhanj was ruled by the Bhanja dynasty. The formation of the kingdom dates back to 1688 with king Sarveswar Bhanja (1688-1711) who was the first ruler of the Bhanja dynasty. Under the Gadajaat king, there were Samant kings who were called Sarvarakars. Sarvarakars were very similar to Zamindars.

They were acting like kings, but they were under the sovereignty of a king. Among those Samant kings of Mayurbhanj, Rairangpur Gadhha was under the reign of Sarvarakar Madhab Das Narendra Mohapatra. Administratively, Mayurbhanj district was divided into two units based on its hilly topography. The Baripada area which is the present district headquarter was one unit and the area beyond the Bamanghaty was another. Baripada was under the administrative control of Medinipore District Collector whereas Bamanghaty was under the Hazaribag Collector. Since Mayurbhanj was divided among two collectors, many law-and-order challenges used to creep in and there was confusion among people owing to the complex nature of governance. Who was the authority? The British Government, the king or the Sarvarakar? The mal-governance of the time and lack of clarity led to a revolt, called the *Praja Meli*, by the subjects. Both Adivasis and Non-Adivasis participated equally in the revolt in order to establish better governance in Mayurbhanj.

During that time, Sarvarakar of Rairangpur, Madhab Das Narendra Mohapatra declared himself king. He brought the subjects under his fold, luring them with tax exemption. This domineering tendency of the Sarvarakar was a matter of concern for the Mayurbhanj Maharaja, Jadunath Bhanj Deo, who reigned from 1828 to 1863. He wrote a letter to the Collector, Medinipore to take action. However, the Collector of Medinipore did not have cordial relations with the Collector of Hazaribag. Hence, he took no action to restore the sovereignty of the king. Finding no alternative, Jadunath Bhanj attacked Bamanghaty. First, he occupied Rairangpur. Then he marched to occupy Tentagarh, (now Tentoposi) and the adjacent village of Uparbeda. In the first inning, the king got defeated. Then the king declared openly that, if he displaced four castes from Bamanghaty, the Santhals would get the landed property. These four castes were Dhuruwa, Gond, Bathudi, and Sounti. This royal declaration led to internal aggression among the communities for survival. Nevertheless, the inter-community war was contained in just a few hours. The inhabitants belonging to these four castes moved out of the Tentoposi area and shifted near Jashipur. Tentoposi had witnessed war in 1835 for the last time. Amongst Uparbeda and the adjoining Edelbeda, Dubulabeda, Baliadhipa, Tentoposi, Rangamatia, the villages Dubulabeda, Baliadhipa and Tentaposi were deserted after the war as the communities shifted from their habitation. All the property of these three villages came under the jurisdiction of Sardar. The Dhuruwa, Gond, Bathudi, and Sounti tribes, who had to leave their villages, developed severe aversion to visit Tentoposi even after two centuries. The repercussions were so strong that, even after centuries, they did not drink water during their visits to these villages.

In the nineteenth century, in Bamanghaty, there lived a Gontiya, a tax collector of 2-3 villages), whose name was Bhaga, Bhagiratha or Bhagat. He was not only a tax collector but also had judicial powers. He would take care of disciplinary issues of the community, protect forest resources, and make developmental decisions for the area. A Gontiya was the conduit between the king and the subjects. It appears that Gontiya Bhagiratha was killed in the Tentoposi war.

The Tentaposi war also led to changes in administration. The appointment of a Gontiya was stopped and a new system of appointing Sardars started. Sardars took charge of bigger geographical units called Peedha. Peedha is a Pargana comprising approximately 52 mouzas (revenue village) and was considered an administrative unit in pre-independent India. Some of the Peedhas of Bamanghaty subdivision are Uparbeda Peedha, Basila Peedha, Jamda Peedha, Khasdesh Peedha, Untudi Peedha etc. Bhagiratha's son Banaju Sardar was the first tribal Sardar of Uparbeda Peedha of Bhamanghaty. Historically, it was quite a significant achievement that a tribal became a Sardar by his own merit. Generally, educated administrators from Kolkata, Katak, or Baleswar used to be the Sardars of the Peedhas in Mayurbhanj. These sardars who were not the sons of the soil would often be imperious and this fomented widespread resentment towards them. In 1852, there was a tribal rebellion to protest the existing practice of nominating Sardars. The king of Mayurbhanj, Maharaja Jadunath Bhanj Deo carried out the investigation and concluded that the Sardars appointed from outside fuelled tribal uprisings. He changed this policy and started appointing Sardars from the same tribal community to contain the conflict. For example, one from Bage clan of Jamada got the opportunity of being a Sardar. Much later, a son of the Bage Sardar family, Bhage Govardhan became a civil servant in the Indian Administrative Service, and later became the Human Resource Development Minister of the country as well. This administrative reform could contain the revolt for some time. However, the governance system was not very robust owing to the presence of multiple authorities.

Due to lack of clear distribution of power, the three power centres viz., the Sardar, the King and the British, continued to create confusion among the masses and fuelled new internal rebellions from time to time. In 1865 Thomas Edward Ravenshaw was appointed Divisional Commissioner of Odisha by the British government, He was posted in Cuttack, the capital of Odisha Province. In 1865, there was a drought which was followed by the great famine in Odisha in 1866 known as *Na Anka Durbhikhya,* (as the famine occurred in the ninth regal year of the king Gajapati Dibyasingha Deb). One third of Odisha's population amounting to 10 million approximately perished in the famine. The discontentment among people aggravated because of the lack of resources which affected their ability to make a living. This happened because the government failed to cater to the needs of the people. Mr. Ravenshaw paid a visit to Tentagarh to douse the rebellion successfully.

In the following year, 1867, the Maharaja of Mayurbhanj, Srinath Bhanj, passed away after being on the throne for just four years since 1863. This led to the coronation of the 22-year-old

Krushna Chandra Bhanj Deo (1867-1882). He was a ruler par excellence and contributed not only to Mayurbhanj but also to the development of Cuttack and Odisha. The king was such a visionary that he donated Rs. 20,000/- as a permanent endowment for the establishment of Ravenshaw College (then Cuttack College) which almost fulfilled the condition imposed by the British Government for public contributions. This is one of the many examples of his valuable contribution to the development of Odisha state.

As regards the local administration of Uparbeda Peedha, Banaju's son Bhagat Tudu succeeded as Sardar after him and he continued in the post till 1890. After him, his son Kartik Chandra Tudu became the Sardar of Uparbeda Peedha who served for a period from 1890 to 1940. He was the longest serving Sardar. The Sardars left a glorious legacy for the people of Uparbeda as they were philanthropic in nature.

The Sardars used to have a jail in their villages as per the judiciary powers bestowed on them. Their bodyguards were called Paikas. Karthik Chandra Tudu would decide judiciary cases at his level and was very lenient when it came to handing out punishments. If the accused had small children or the spouse requested for pardon, he used to free the accused by granting pardon. If he thought that he could not pardon the guilty, the accused was sent to Gujuri Bazaar Jail in Baripada. He distributed land to the landless and home to the homeless. These citizen-friendly administrative initiatives benefited the people and made him immensely popular among them. The philanthropic legacy of sardars was continued by his successors even after the abolition of the post of Sardar. The Sardars distributed thousands of acres of land to establish new communities. Through the process of 'Aman Nama' (lease deed), the land records were created in the name of the land holder in the court of the Mayurbhanj king in Baripada. Taxes were levied to the land holders. Karthik Chandra's son Bhagat Charan Tudu became the sardar after him. It was during his tenure, that the country attained political independence making him officially the last Sardar of Uparbeda. Mayurbhanj became an independent princely state after independence. On 1 January 1949, during the reign of king Paratap Chandra Bhanjdeo, it was acceded to the Union of India and became a part of Orissa province, which eventually became the state of Odisha.

Uparbeda: Ancestral village of Droupadi Tudu

Within a timespan of approximately two centuries, the Sardar families of Uparbeda have grown to become 40-45 households. Many families are living outside Uparbeda and some family members are engaged in jobs. Some families have sold their properties in the village to settle in the cities in search of good education for the new generation and in search of greener pastures. In recent times, the descendants of the Sardar family have expanded to approximately 30-35 families. No one among them is landless. Bhagat Narayan Tudu had approximately 30 acres of land. During his time, he sold some portion of the property. However, his three sons, Biranchi, Ananta and Banaju, inherited not less than 20 acres of landed property in Uparbeda and adjacent Edelbeda.

After the abolition of the post of Sardar, Bhagat Charan Tudu shifted to Edelbeda and started living there with his family. However, on the creation of a new post of Pradhan or Mukhiya for the village headman, the villagers invited Bhagat to hold the post. Bhagat agreed and shifted to Uparbeda again. After him, his eldest son Biranchi Narayan Tudu became the village headman. He was also called *Halam baba*, etymologically the oldest person in Santalis. The *Halam Baba* would perform rituals, conduct marriages, and mediate for conflict resolution, among other things in the village. Biranchi's personality influenced all the villagers. To become a Halam Baba, one needs the support and faith of all villagers, which he had. After the abolition of the post of Pradhan, Biranchi worked as a team member of the Panchayati Raj Department of the state, though he was not a government employee. He prepared the necessary documentation for the office. He got a nominal stipend of Rs 20/ or Rs. 30/- during that time. Biranchi was not an elected Panchayat representative, but he used to take care of the village like a head man even though there were no formal designations. He was involved in almost all the developmental work, especially that which pertained to education. He was also the convener of the entertainment programme, viz., Chhau Dance of the village, a semi-classical, tribal, martial dance form practiced in the Eastern states of the country.

In the year 1958, Uparbeda and many nearby villages witnessed sporadic rainfall in the first part of May. However, the locality did not witness monsoon either in the later part of May or till mid-June like every year. The Raja festival which falls on the 13, 14, and 15 June witnessed unprecedented dry days. The lack of rain fall increased the concern of the farmers as paddy is an important crop and the backbone of their survival. The oppressive heat in the tropical region led to drought conditions. In desperation, the farmers started cultivation in the hope of rainfall. People of different faiths were found worshipping their *Aradhya debata (*Deity of worship). Some villagers began reading the Ramayan. It was believed that it rains when the chapter of Rishi Rishyasringa (deer-horned' sage in Sanskrit) was read. The legend goes like this. Rishi Rishyasringa was the son of Rishi Vibhandaka and his celestial paramour Menaka. Vibhandaka was a renowned sage and was son of Kashyapa. Menaka left the newborn son with his father and went back to her celestial abode. Hence, Rishi Rishyashringa was raised in the forest, and he had never seen any woman in his life being protected by Rishi Vibhandaka. When he grew up as a young man, there was the kingdom of Anga, which suffered from drought and famine. The king, Romapada (Lompada), was advised ways to get rid of the extreme weather conditions by performing Yagyas by a chaste brahmin. The only such person available was Rishi Rishyasringa. He was then brought to the city and was persuaded to carry out the necessary ceremonies. As envisaged by the king, Rishyasringa used his powers and knowledge to grant rainfall in the kingdom. The kingdom received plenty of rain that season. Later on, Rishyasringa got married to Shanta, the princess and daughter of king Romapada.

The offering started in the Jaher Garh of Uparbeda Peedha, the sacred place of worship for Santhals. Placing of sacred *Kalasha* or *Ghata* (earthen pot for worship), offerings and Sankirthan (devotional group singing) were carried out in the Kamala Bimala Temple near Bhagat's home. The Gramya devi (Goddess of the village), Kamala Bimala Goddess was also known as *Kala Darni Aaya* (Auspicious mother divine) in Santali. Moreover, Kamala is the name of Mahalaxmi, cohort of Lord Jagannath and Bimla is *Aadi Mata* (primordial mother divine) and cohort of Lord

Balabhadra. In the temple, the villagers would perform animal sacrifices twice in a year for better harvest and rainfall. *Nuakhia Janthal* (a tribal festival) is one such occasion. Normally, the villagers offer worship once a week under the guidance of the priest known as the *Dehuri*. However, if someone vows (*Manasika*) then *Dehuri* visits the temple more frequently to perform the rituals. The veneration in *Sindhukeswar Shiva* temple at the entry of the village was also in full swing. Pujas and offerings were carried out in four different places simultaneously to appease the main God to save the crops. On the mountain of Uparbeda, the Budharana Pata Devata (deity) is worshiped, once again, demonstrating the rich culture of venerating mother nature.

Kamala Bimla Temple adjacent to the ancestral home of Droupadi Tudu in Uparbeda village, Bamanghaty subdivision, Mayurbhanj district of Odisha

It was a Friday morning on 20 June 1958 at 11.45 AM, when the entire village was totally engrossed in the fervour of devotion to the almighty, that an angel in the form of a female baby was born in Sardar family to Biranchi Narayan Tudu and Singo Tudu, granddaughter to Bhagat Charan Tudu and Sunamani Tudu. As per Vedic astrology, this baby was born on the most auspicious day having Pushya Nakshatra which is the part of Karkata Rashi (Cancer Zodiac sign) during Kanya Lagna wherein Brihaspati (Jupiter) was sitting in it. The position of other stars was that Ravi-Budh (Sun-Mercury) was in the 10th House and Mangal (Mars) in the 7th house, which predicted the newborn baby to be a bright child. According to western astrology, she was a Gemini depicting a quick-witted and cheerful character. Green, yellow and orange are the lucky colours of Gemini. In Santhal culture and tradition, the children are named after their grandparents. This is also in vogue in some parts of the south Indian states. In that analogy, the eldest baby girl would have to be named as Sunamani after her grandmother. However, in this case, the baby girl was named 'Durgi' after the name of her aunt (sister of her father) who had had an untimely demise. Subsequently, Durgi was called by her pet name Puti in the household.

Ancestral home where Droupadi Tudu was born in the Uparbeda village, Bamanghaty subdivision, Mayurbhanj district of Odisha

Few elders in the village opine that Puti's birth was a week before the 20 June 1958. However, no concrete evidence to the fact is found. The news of the birth of a girl child spread immediately. The parents started calling her Puti (meaning daughter and beads prepared from glass). Puti was a sweet toddler, and she brought a lot of joy to the big joint family. Her grandparents were from a respected lineage, and she imbibed family etiquette. She demonstrated composed demeanour from her childhood.

Puti's father was the Mukhiya of the village. The Mukhiya or a Pradhan or a village headman would give judgment on local issues, family conflict and look into the development of the village. Her lineage as has been discussed not only speaks about the legacy of indigenous Sardars of Uparbeda but how the family influenced the socio-political life of the people positively. Her grandfather and father continued to be the village headmen and commanded great respect. Puti's mother Singo was a beautiful lady with a charming persona. Her father was also tall, dark and handsome. The couple was a perfect match for each other. There is a fascinating story behind the marriage of Singo and Biranchi. Once Bhagat saw a beautiful 10-year-old girl playing in the sand in her village. Bhagat enquired about the parents of the girl and expressed his desire to make the girl his daughter-in-law. He was expecting beautiful grandchildren in the future. Singo was poor. Her father agreed to the proposal, thus the marriage of Singo and Biranchi was solemnised. Singo became a child bride and came to her in-laws when she was just ten years old. Bhagat and Sunamani's son Biranchi was a very precious child to his parents. Unfortunately, his parents had lost all eleven children born to them before him. So, when he was born, his parents sold him to a family in the neighbourhood as the last recourse to save the child as per the social belief of those times. The ritual was customary, because after the end of the process, the child could stay with his biological parent. He was called Ghasiram in his childhood according to the caste of the family he was sold to. This might look like a blind belief to the scientific mind, but the couple were happy to save their child and thankfully he did live long.

Puti was not born to the landless poor, but the circumstances of the time made her family witness poverty. Puti was the eldest daughter in the family. She was very fond of her mother like most children. She was immensely influenced by her grandmother who was her role model. Sunamani had very good knowledge on wellbeing and healthy living. She helped the villagers in many ways. Puti was a bright child and also very calm and composed. She would follow her mother everywhere. Her father had high aspirations for her. She used to sit beside her father when he delivered certain decisions on community issues as a head man of the village in the place called Darbar. She was an adorable child in the village because of her composure and adaptability. She would show interest in books and study materials even as a toddler. She would draw pictures everywhere with the colourful stones available in the courtyard. Those days, the Santhals decorated their houses with different colours by procuring coloured stones and mud from the mountain. The houses were made of mud and thatched roofs and kept extremely clean The exterior was immaculately painted by the family members. Colourful tribal paintings with various motifs would make the houses look beautiful. Puti fetched colours and mud with her grandmother from the foothills of the mountain. Her tiny hand curled inside her grandmother's protective hands; she went with zeal to watch the bountiful nature. She was often amazed to see nature's abundance and her inquisitive mind asked many questions. Her parents answered those patiently.

Puti was growing, bringing a lot of pride and joy to the household. Her youngest uncle, Banaju Tudu would take her to show her the immaculate make-up he would do for various historical characters in the theatre, Chhau dance, and Jhumar dance in the village. She would be bewildered to see different characters decked up in kaleidoscopic attire, their facial expressions, and ornaments. He used to dress like a *Bahurupi* (harlequin) as well. The *Bahurupi* attracted many village kids who would queue up marvelling at his act and were fascinated by various characters.

Come winter, one of the biggest agrarian festivals of the area Makar Sankranti also known as Makar Parab and Sakrat is observed with much pomp and ceremony after the harvest of paddy. It falls on the Indian month of *Pausa* and in the Gregorian calendar of mid-January every year. The festival is also called Uttarayan as from Makar Sankranti (14 January) the sun begins its northward journey ushering in the pleasant weather, and mother nature's bountifulness. People worship the Sun God and offer *Makar Chaula* (rice) as part of the rituals. Even though it's a three-day festival, the Santhal society observes the festival for a week in myriad hues and by preparing *Arisa Pitha*, Puti's favourite cuisine. *Arisa Pitha* is made up of jaggery, rice and oil. Some well-to-do households use ghee instead of oil. *Handia* (Home brew made of rice) is prepared by every Santhal household for the occasion. Not only tribals but most of the inhabitants especially Kudumi-Mohanta of Odisha, Jharkhand, and West Bengal observe *Makar Parab* with much fanfare. The villagers feast on mudhi (puffed rice), meat, Handia and *Arisa pitha* during the festival. The villagers paint their houses and bring new clothes from nearby *haat* (local market) to wear.

Tusu is the name of the Goddess worshiped by the villagers prior and during Makar Sankanti. The villagers carrying the *Tusu* idol, visit all the households singing *Tusu* songs. Many Tusu songs have also been composed in a lighter vein in Kudumi-Mohanta dialect cognizant with the contemporary lifestyle. One of the famous *Tusu* song of childhood memory which can fondly be recalled goes like this, *"Digdo dido Makar Parabe. Toke ke delare Lal Sadhhi, Chingdi Machhara Hilailo Dadhi"* (In the festivity of Makar Parab, who has given you the red saree? You have shaken the beard of a prawn.) Some songs are composed to match the preceding lines rhythmically and may carry an altogether different connotation. The *Tusu* dance is also very famous, wherein the men move in clockwise direction and the women in an anti-clockwise direction. Mostly unmarried boys and girls congregate at one place to dance after having their ceremonial bath in the river before their performance. Normally, the dance is performed in groups with simple steps without any accompanying musical instrument. The month of festivity witnesses a lot of cultural and sports activities viz., performance of *Chhau* dance and Jhumair or Jhumar dance (folk dance), Jhumair songs, etc. in the evenings. Some fire poles (*mashals*) are kept in the area where Chhau dance is performed for the purpose of lighting. The villages hold football matches, *Kukuda Padha* (cock fights) and various sports competitions. Goats, cocks, metal utensils are distributed as prizes to the winners. At the end of these events all the villagers congregate for a common feast with the prizes they received called 'Prize *Khia'* (community feast on winning prizes).

Tusu Mela or *Tusu Jatra* happens in Baliadhipa village on 16th and 17th of January every year. The celebrations seem to be never ending in tribal villages. The celebration is a sign of the mature understanding of tribal societies about leading a happy life. This is followed by the Hindu month of Magha and in it, the Saraswati Pooja, an important festival for students is observed in educational institutions.

Saraswati Pooja (worship of the Goddess Mother Saraswati, the bestower of Education) or *Vasant Panchami* is observed in educational institutions of Odisha with much festivity and dedication. On the fifth day of the Hindu month *Magha*, *Vasant* (spring) sets in. Generally, a big classroom or open place is allocated for the Pooja. Students and teachers decorate the place of worship with coloured papers and mango leaves, flowers, rangoli etc. Students get up early in the morning to pluck flowers and make a big garland for the goddess. At around 10 AM, the *Nana/ pujari* (priest) comes to perform the Pooja. The students offer *Pushpanjali* (offer flower) to the Goddess, break a coconut, and offer *Aarati*. After completion of the *Pooja* in approximately two hours, all students sit together for the *Prasad Sevana* (devotional offering made to the Goddess shared by all later) in the school. These are memorable occasions for every child in school.

In 1963, Basudeb Behera, a student of class five who became a teacher in the Uparbeda M.E. School in later years took the responsibility of organising the Saraswati Pooja in the Uparbeda upper primary school. He along with his classmates would start the preparation a few days ahead of the day of the Pooja. The headmaster Madan Mohan Mohanta and assistant teacher Harihar Mishra would guide them. Harihar Mishra was a Brahmin who could also conduct the Pooja as a priest. Every student would contribute by bringing one bowl of raw rice (Arua Chaula) and one bowl of par-boiled rice (Usuna Chaula). The rich students would bring one kilogram or more of rice. Hence, during the festival 50-60 kilograms of rice would be collected. The Prasad would be prepared with that rice. Some portions were offered to the priest and the teachers and used as Dakshina. Puti's Vidyarambh ceremony (commencement of education popularly known as *Khadi Chhua* in Odisha) took place on Vasant Panchami on 29 January 1963. It was a slightly chilly day in Upadbeda at the end of winter.

Droupadi's teacher Basudeb Behera and his wife Somlata Behera from their home at Tentoposi village, Bamanghaty Sub-Division, Mayurbhanj, Odisha. Basudeb was in Class V during Puti's Vidyarambh ceremony Uparbeda U.P. School

Biranchi Narayan's cousin Karna Tudu was an accomplished artist. He used to prepare masks for the characters viz., Lord Rama, Lord Krishna, Radhika, Sita etc for the Chhau Tribal martial dance held every year in the village. Karna was young and dynamic and was an alumnus of Uparbeda upper primary school. He offered his expertise to make the idol (Moorti) of Mata Saraswati in mud and colour at his own cost as many boys and girls of the village were starting their education (Vidyarambha ceremony) on that auspicious day of Vasant Panchami. This was appreciated by Biranchi Narayan, who was also the president of the school as well as the Halam Baba of the village.

Karna made a beautiful big earthen idol using the colours viz., white, yellow, black, red etc. available in the village. He made one swan (*Harmsa*), the carrier (*Vahan*) of the Goddess and a peacock. Such a huge creation needed a lot of clothes. The students collected all the old clothes, used for the purpose. However, the size of the swan became very huge which made it look like a vulture to many. A talkative gentleman of the village, named Beni Majhi had jocularly said to Karna, "Where did you get the old vulture?" Listening to the comment, the simpleton Karna Tudu wept unstoppably. However, Biranchi Narayan came to his rescue saying that he should not be a victim of other people's opinions. He told Karna the Panchatantra narrative of *Tini Tundare Chheli Kukura* (an Odia proverb meaning a lie told multiple times has the ability to be perceived as truth). Though he did not reprimand Beni for his mindless comment, this example made Beni realize his fault for dampening others' enthusiasm. Beni realized his mistake by apologizing and crying. At the end, Biranchi Narayan pacified both and asked them to conduct the worship amicably with the cooperation of all.

Puti along with many boys and girls had her Vidyarambha on 29 January 1963 on a Tuesday morning of Vasant Panchami. Harihar Mishra, guided Puti to write Brahma, Vishnu and Maheswar on the slate, with the chalk for the first time. Puti's flawless pronunciation in Odia surprised many. Biranchi Narayan was pleased to see this, and said that since the children of Giri family, Mohanty family and Tudu family play together, all had picked up speaking Odia and Santhali equally well. Harihar Mishra kept the official good names of many students on that day. These names were inspired by scriptures and Puranas viz., Droupadi, Parvati, Menaka, Urvasi, Sita. Puti got a new name as Droupadi on that day. Puti became the nickname to be called by family and Droupadi, the good name and school name, thereafter. However, her peers and acquaintances could not pronounce the name properly and she was called Drupati, Durpati etc. gradually to Droupadi. Droupadi in a new surrounding was thrilled to take part in the Prasad Sevana (community feast with the food offered to the deity) along with all the students at the school. It was her first interaction in the school on the auspicious day, full of festivity and grandeur.

Droupadi Tudu enrolled for *Shishu Shreni* in Uparbeda upper primary school that day and from the following day, started going to school accompanied by her father. The next day of the Pooja was observed as the *Visarjan* (immersion of the idol after worship) of the deity in the water reservoir. A few senior students escorted by the teacher did the honour in the nearest pond. This was quite an emotional moment especially for many who were in the final year of school. After this year, they would either go to another school for higher education or stop further studies. The village did not have any education facility beyond class seven. Uparbeda Middle English school would impart education for class six and seven. After that, one had to travel or be a residential student in Rairangpur High School which was 14 kilometres away. Everyone in the community had to cross the Kanhu River. If one was commuting by bicycle it had to be carried through the river braving mud in summer and water in the rains. These villages were bounded by the Kanhu River towards the east and mountains and the Jharkhand state towards the west. The nearest *haat* (weekly fair) was Hatbadla. The residents of the village had to take a turn at

Kaduani in Hatbadla- Rairangpur road. There was no vehicle going to the village as there was no bridge on the Kanhu River. People who were coming from outside had to get down at Kaduani and walk 7-9 kilometres to reach Uparbeda, Dubulabeda, Baliadhipa and Tantaposi villages. Due to lack of communication facilities from the villages, the students had no option but to stop education unless one was a brilliant student.

Kanhu river flowing between Kaduani Chhak and Uparbeda village

Biranchi Narayan had two wives. His second wife Sunamani Tudu had two children, one daughter named Sita Tudu and one son named Bhagat Charan Tudu. There were two Bhagats who were half-brothers. Looking back 200 years in history, it is evident that every second generation had a Bhagat. Biranchi's younger brothers Ananta and Banaju had also two wives totalling six daughters-in-law in the family as there were three sons of Bhagat. Puti's grandfather Bhagat Narayan Tudu had also two wives. Perhaps this was a social order of the time when polygamy was practiced in society. However, these family members of the Sardar ancestry lived peacefully in one household for quite a long time. They never fought among themselves and set a benchmark of good etiquette.

Now the ancestral home of Droupadi has been renovated, and her nephew Dularam Tudu stays with his wife Dulari and two children Chuda Sakra and Bhagat Shyam. Her sister-in-law (*Bhauja*) Chudamani Tudu and the mother of Dularam stays with another son Biranchi Narayan Tudu and his wife Jasmine Tudu and two grandsons Taranisen and Bhagat Charan in a nearby hamlet called Dunguri Sahi.

The genealogy of Droupadi Tudu till 2022 is enumerated in the book.

Droupadi's nephew Dularam, his wife Dulari and children Chuda Sakra and Bhagat Shyam in the ancestral home Uparbeda village

Jaher Garh in Kaduani adjacent to Uparbeda village

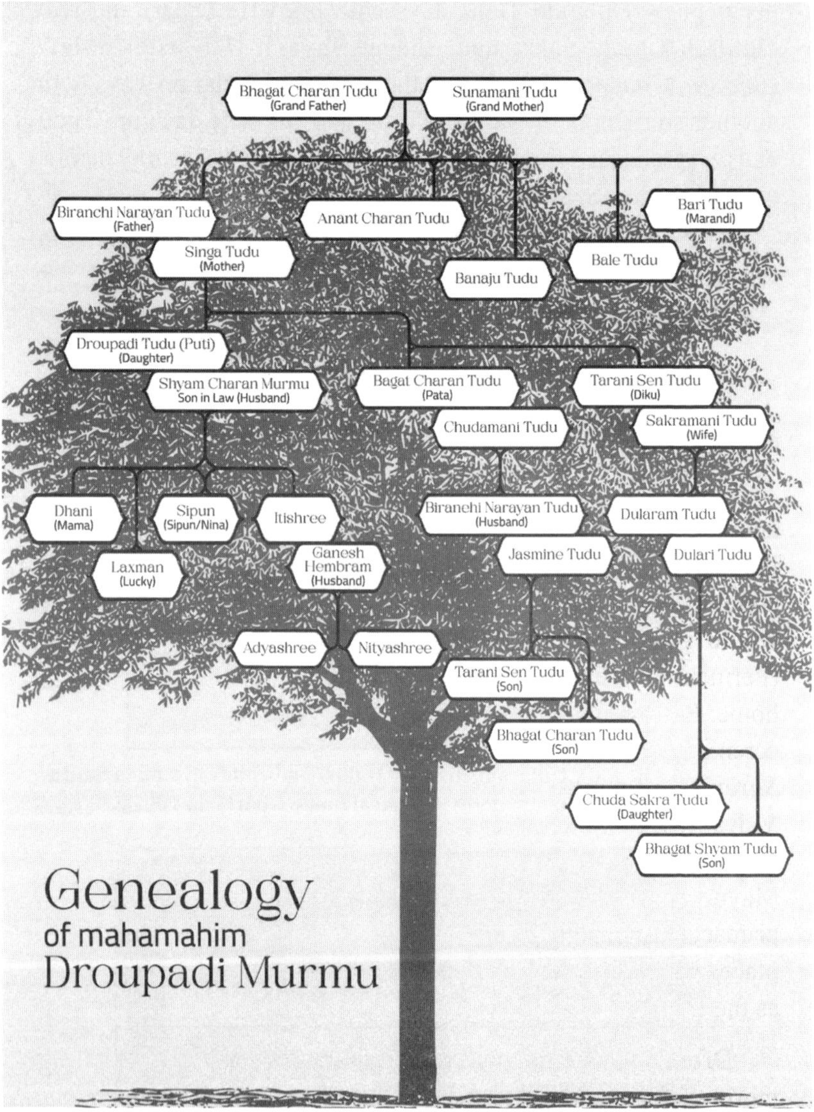
Bhagat Charan Tudu (Grand Father)
Sunamani Tudu (Grand Mother)
Biranchi Narayan Tudu (Father)
Singa Tudu (Mother)
Anant Charan Tudu
Banaju Tudu
Bale Tudu
Bari Tudu (Marandi)
Droupadi Tudu (Puti) (Daughter)
Shyam Charan Murmu Son in Law (Husband)
Bagat Charan Tudu (Pata)
Chudamani Tudu
Tarani Sen Tudu (Diku)
Sakramani Tudu (Wife)
Dhani (Mama)
Laxman (Lucky)
Sipun (Sipun/Nina)
Itishree
Ganesh Hembram (Husband)
Adyashree
Nityashree
Biranchi Narayan Tudu (Husband)
Jasmine Tudu
Tarani Sen Tudu (Son)
Bhagat Charan Tudu (Son)
Dularam Tudu
Dulari Tudu
Chuda Sakra Tudu (Daughter)
Bhagat Shyam Tudu (Son)
Genealogy
of mahamahim
Droupadi Murmu

Chapter - 2

Formative Years: Exploring the Early Education and Schooling (1963-70)

It dawns early for the people of Uparbeda as they go to bed early and rise early. Many villagers in India do the same.

The houses in the village are lined up in two rows facing one another. A *kaccha* (unmetalled) road lies in between, which gets inundated in the rainy season making it difficult for neighbours to commute even a distance of 100 feet. The farmers and labourers would go to the paddy field and work after having *Pakhala* (Fermented rice in water), and *Sajana Saga* (Moringa leaves) at home. Puti with her new name Droupadi (after the *Vidyarambha* ceremony), started going to school from 30 January 1963 as a *Sishu Shreni* (Pre-primary class) of Uparbeda Uccha Prathamika Vidyalaya (Upper Primary School) which was established in 1902 near her ancestral home. The popular educationist king of Mayurbhanj Sri Ram Chandra Bhanj Deo constructed 20 lower primary (L.P.) schools in Bamanghaty. Uparbeda is one the 20 places where a school was established. Later on, it was renamed as the Uparbeda U.P. School.

Droupadi was excited to begin school on a chilly winter morning. She wore the new frock which was bought from the Hatbadla *Haat* by her father Biranchi for Makar Sankranti. She rushed to the neighbour Malati Giri, whom she would call grandmother to tie her hair and make a bun with a white ribbon. She walked down cheerfully to the school with her father. She saw colourful butterflies and (dragon flies) on the way. The school was located in a scenic and serene place with a pond nearby. Charming creepers with pink flowers surrounded the pond adding more beauty to the place. *Sadhaba Bohu* (Trombidiidae or Red velvet Mite) shows up in the rainy season. Some students would throw pebbles to see the ripples in water. In the middle of the pond, the top portion of a big stone would make an isle of approximately 24 inches. Two cranes would sit and make their daily meal plan of fish and other insects. The resplendent beauty and abundance of nature in the village was a boon of nature's bounty. Whether to be grateful for this or not was up to the human being.

Festivities are synonymous with tribal cultural heritage. Village life is full of colours, camaraderie, and celebrations. In the Gregorian calendar, on 15th of April falls the Maha Bishuba Sankranti, the Odia New year. It is customary to suspend an earthen pot (*theki*) filled with water having a hole at the bottom above the *Tulasi Chaura* (Basil plant) in the courtyard. This marks the commencement of the hot summer. It also saves the basil plant from the scorching heat. *Chhatua* (*Sattu* or the powdered pulses) is offered to the deity and is served as Prasad to all. *Bela Pana* (Stone Apple juice) is prepared on the occasion and is distributed to all. The day is also known as *Chhatua* Sankranti and *Pana* Sankranti as well. The offerings in the festivals are very symbolic and scientific, considering the prevailing weather conditions and geography. The tribals observe *Udaa Parva* on that day.

In *Udaa Parva* some people of the village observe severe penance. Some walk on fire, some pierce the body and hang on a rope that passes through the body. The euphoria and the energy of the time are unmatched and need to be seen to be believed. The tribals are not only hard working but have immense faith in the Almighty. Needless to say, they are not affected physically even though it all looks extremely torturous to watch. The spiritual energy protects the believer. The *Chaitra Parva* is also marked by the Chhau festival, which is celebrated for three consecutive days on 13, 14, and 15 April. This has been patronized since the rule of the *Bhanja* kings.

The new academic year started in June 1963. After studying there for only three months, Droupadi was promoted to Class 1 as she was intelligent. This made her the youngest girl in the new class. Her father Biranchi was the President of the Uparbeda U.P. School and the Secretary in Uparbeda Madhya Ingrazi Vidyalaya (Middle English School). As a *Halam Baba* (etymologically an elderly person designated to be headman/Mukhiya/ Pradhan of the village), he was highly respected in the village. Every day, he would visit both the schools to enquire about the welfare of the schools. The visionary Biranchi Narayan Tudu along with other committee members used to discuss the upliftment of the school and how to upgrade those model institutions. As a result, Uparbeda U.P. School and M.E. School created many records of the time. There used to be a boys' hostel in the U.P. School which attracted many students from distant villages. He would check with the teachers about the academic progress of his daughter. This was very progressive thinking for those times. Many girls of her age did not get an opportunity to be educated. However, it was the *Sankalpa* (intention) of the Tudu Sardar family to educate girls. Six acres of land was donated by Karthik Majhi, grandson of Karthik Sardar of Sardar family for the construction of Uparbeda U.P. school which included a picturesque pond with flowering plants surrounding the pond. Similarly, four acres of land was donated by the villagers for the formation of the M.E. School.

Government Upper Primary School, Uparbeda, in Bamanghaty Subdivision of Mayurbhanj District, where Droupadi Tudu completed her Primary Education

Picturesque water reservoir in front of Government Upper Primary School in Uparbeda

As a new student, the young Droupadi would be amazed to see the beauty of the flowers and the ripples in the pond as she walked to school every day with her father. The flora and fauna were mesmerizing and so was the demeanour of the contented and smiling people. If anyone wants to understand contentment, camaraderie, and happiness, one should visit the village where people of different caste, creed and faith live like *Vasudhaiva Kutumbakam* (the world is one family).

The child Droupadi was no exception. She was brought up not only by her parents but also by the extended family and the neighbouring Giri (*Gopal*) and Mohanty (*Karana*) families. Malati Giri would tie for Droupadi, her favourite white ribbons in her hair, whereas her friend Tapati Mandal would tie red ribbons for her. Malati's own eldest granddaughter Rebati who was 2-3 years younger than Droupadi could not go to school as the family was going through abject poverty due to the untimely demise of Malati's son. Rebati and her three younger brothers would often be in

Tapati Mandal (1st from left), Droupadi's friend in Upper Primary School with her family & acquaintances, Uparbeda village, Bamanghaty Subdivision of Mayurbhanj District

Droupadi's home and were helped by her family. Rebati reminisces emotionally that, "My three brothers and I were raised by the Tudu family. Droupadi's mother Singo was not only a good-looking lady but also had a golden heart. When I was 12 years old with three younger brothers, my father passed away. I cannot recollect the face of my father because we were so poor that we did not possess even a photograph of him."

Droupadi was born in a Sardar family which owned cultivable land of approximately 25 acres which belonged to her grandfather. Her grandfather Bhagat and his three sons Biranchi, Ananta, and Banaju each had two wives. They coexisted peacefully and had cordial relations with one another. The big joint family and increasing members of the family put a lot of financial pressure on the household. When Droupadi was five-year old, her two uncles Ananta and Banaju parted ways, dividing the property. This weakened the economic condition of the household. Moreover, there was drought for the next 2-3 years which was a big jolt to agrarian families like hers. Eventually their economic condition worsened.

When she was in Class 1, Madan Mohan Mohanta was the Headmaster or Head Pandit of the school. Prabhakra Mohanta, Basanta Giri and Harihar Mishra from Cuttack were the other three teachers. When she was in class IV, the teachers at the schools were Raghunath Das (Headmaster), Gobinda Majhi, Hrushikesh Bhuyan, and Sushen Giri of Baliadhipa village. Gourahari Giri was teaching *Chatashali* (nursery). Toddlers and children would fondly address him as 'Kaka' (uncle). Subsequently, when the school was taken up by the government, it was found that he did not possess adequate qualifications to become a teacher even though he taught many students with his marvellous teaching prowess. However, for procuring a salary and pensionary benefits for the government school, he was posted as an office assistant. He would clean the school being a responsible office assistant. Seeing this, Droupadi and a few of her friends would come to the school early and clean the classrooms so that Gourahari did not have to sweep as he was teaching alphabets and numerical to many students including her. This shows a heightened *Sanskar* (moral norms) of the people living in the village.

When Droupadi was in Class 5, Bijaya Kumar Giri, elder brother of her teacher Basanta Giri, became the headmaster. Basanta Giri was a Minor Education Teacher (MET) who taught Droupadi social science, history, *Swasthya Raksha* (Health and Well-being) in her classes four and five. He was getting a salary of Rs. 40/- per month as a non-governmental employee. Later, the Government took up the school and regularized the salary. Now he gets a monthly pension of more than Rs.18,000/-.

Basant Giri said, "During those days, teacher-students and guardians were aligned very strongly. This enabled the teachers to impart quality education and students to learn attentively. There would be so much respect for teachers. Anyone who taught well was made a teacher. In due course, the qualifications, trainings were added as a prerequisite to be posted as a teacher by the Government,"

Droupadi kept herself busy with her studies. In the morning and in the evening, she would go to *Chatsali* for extra classes. Often, she would stay in the home of her teacher Madan Mohan Mohanta along with her friends Tapati and Kanaklata to study beyond class hours. Kanaklata's father was also her teacher. Madan Sir taught her like he taught his own son. Often, she would stay with his wife and son. She even went along with the family to attend the marriage of his nephew. The bonding among students and teachers would be so strong those days.

Many times, when she was outside her home, her friends would play pranks and would like to scare her by pretending to be ghosts and making scary sounds. Even though she would relate these incidents to her teachers, she would never reveal their names as they were likely to be punished. She was a good friend to girls as well as boys in the class. She was called naughty as she played with boys and often defeated them. However, this was an affectionate term used in the village for energetic & playful children.

Droupadi and her friends would get bamboo sticks from their village. She would cut these into small sizes, and sharpen them to be used as pens. She would use green ink prepared from *Jhudanga* (cowpea) leaves. In certain rare occasions, an ink pot would be purchased from the Hatbadla weekly *haat* and she and her friends would use that. There were no fountain pens or ball pens available in the village. She took this as a challenge and continued to excel in academia. She would make opportunities from adversities by her dedication, sincerity, and intelligence. Someone has said that you must be comfortable with being uncomfortable, that is when you became unstoppable. She was destined to grow despite hailing from one of the remotest, and inaccessible parts of the nation.

Droupadi was appearing for the Odia Mother Indian Language abbreviated as MIL examination in the M.E. school. One question was to find out common names of the characters depicted in the Mahabharat. For example, the question would come, who is *Dhananjay* or *Gudakesh* or *Partha*. The answer to it is *Arjun*. Similarly, *Dharmaraj* or *Kanka* are the alternate names of *Yudhisthira*. Droupadi wrote answers to these characters. However, she did not know who *Jagyaseni* was! She was thinking about the same and then the teacher invigilator curiously asked her, 'what happened? Are the questions very tough? Are you able to answer?' Droupadi said, I am not able to recollect who *Jagyaseni* in Mahabharat is? The teacher smilingly said, 'if you do not know the answer, you can write your name.' She could not understand the pun at that time. Later, when she came to know that *Jagyaseni* is another name of Droupadi, she had a hearty laugh and would often quote this example to her family and friends. One who can laugh at one's own mistakes can be invincible.

Droupadi's friend, Tapati Mandal reminisces, she would sing the last line of Robert Frost's poem, "Stopping by the woods on a snowy evening" in Odia followed by *Vande Mataram* and Jai Hind. The couplet was translated to be taught to students in Odia literature and was taught in the textbook in class five those days.

> *"Andhara jetiki aloka setiki ehi je gahana bana,*
> *Tenu tu apanaa sankalpe Achala atala rahare mana;*
> *Agare padichhi patha bahudura ahuri kete je baki,*
> *Chalibi chalibi na padibi thaki mudiba aagaru aakhi."*

(In this deep forest, there is light and darkness in equal proportions. So, you should stay determined and steadfast in your promises. There is a long path ahead and there is a lot to cover. I shall keep on walking and shall not tire before I sleep).

As a child, Droupadi would sing it often. The last stanza of the same famous poem is "The woods are lovely, dark and deep, but I have promises to keep and miles to go before I sleep, and miles to go before I sleep." These lines inspired a generation of leaders like Bharat's first prime minister Jawaharlal Nehru who would keep Robert Frost's book of poems who had the last two lines of this poem written in block letters and placed on his desk as a reminder of his responsibilities.

When Droupadi was asked by her friend, why she was always humming the poem and whether she would like to be a political leader like Prime Minister Jawaharlal Nehru, she would reply that she would go wherever her destiny leads her.

Tapati's cousin Kanakalata was studying in the same class. Kanakalata's father Jugal Kishore Mandal was also a teacher in the same school where Droupadi, Tapati and Kanakalata were studying. Droupadi would stay back after the school hours to clear any doubts she had about the lessons taught that day. Sometimes, they would gather in the evening for extra classes around a lantern. The school had a hostel. However, Uparbeda and fifteen villages nearby did not have any school to study for classes six and seven. Geographically, the west side of the village is surrounded by mountains leading to Jharkhand state, the east side has the Kanhu River which had no bridge. Due to these two obstacles, not many students from the village opted for higher education. The number of female students in school was very low. A few girls who were studying in the UP School were not able to study beyond class five.

In 1952, seven Pradhans of seven villages under Uparbeda Gram Panchayat decided to open a Middle English school as girls of the village were deprived of education after completing class five in the upper primary school. Four acres of land were donated by the Sardar family. This land was at an equal distance from all these four villages of the panchayat. However, the place was amidst cultivation land and there was no *kachha* or *pucca* road to approach the school. Students and teachers used to go to school enroute the paddy fields along the farm bunds (*Billa Hida)*.

Haradev Tiriya was the then MLA of Rairangpur Legislative constituency. People briefed him about the educational needs of the locality. Hence, in 1954 with the efforts of villagers, the Middle English school for class VI and VII was set up. Government supported the initiative granting INR 2000/- and INR 5000/- in the first and second phases respectively to build the school. The residence of Haradev Tiriya was in *Bada Hatana Beda* (Big Sal Tree in Santali) village, only 12 kilometres from Uparbeda. From his place 50 bullock carts of wood were brought to construct the school. Half of the wood was given to the school and the other half was spent as the honourarium of the transport and the labour to all the good Samaritans who brought the wood. Many youth volunteered service (*shram daan)* for the school. Hence, three spacious rooms, two classrooms and one office could be constructed to begin with. From the wood, chair, table, almirah, racks, stools, 60 desks etc. and necessary furniture for the school could be made by the villagers. Later, Government of Odisha granted INR 4000/- for construction of two more rooms and opening of a craft section. Craft education was a unique feature for the schools of those times. Furthermore, one girl's common room, three big rooms and a kitchen were constructed for the Boys' Hostel. Boy students used to stay in the hostel and students from nearby villages chose this school because of the zeal and belongingness demonstrated by the various stakeholders to build it. A few students would stay in their relative's place nearby. The school would impart holistic education. Along with studies, there were provisions for football, volleyball, and other village sports. For poor meritorious students, study materials was provided from the school bank which was created to help the needy. The bank would collect old study materials viz., books, geometry boxes etc. Some students helped in cooking and simultaneously completed their education in the school.

MLA Haradeb Tiriya's younger brother Kishore Chandra Tiriya, a brilliant student of that time had passed B.Sc. from Calcutta University. Though he was extremely erudite, he used to stammer. Hence, he was not willing to work anywhere. He became the first headmaster of the school, working voluntarily without any salary in 1954. From 1955, he would get a salary applicable for Government aided schools, an amount lesser than the Government school teachers which is two-third of the basic pay and eighty percent dearness allowance (DA). Later, there were few more changes made to the rules by the Government.

There was a rivulet in between Uparbeda M.E. school and Droupadi's home. In the academic year 1968-69 she joined as a student of class six in that school. When Droupadi was in class six, Bisweswar Mohanta was transferred and posted as the headmaster of the school along with Dibakar Patra and Jagabandhu Majhi as the assistant teachers at the school. Bisweswar Mohanta hailed from the adjacent village Dubulabeda. He was a student of the first batch in Uparbeda M.E. School taught by Kishore Chandra Tiriya. He passed class seven in the year 1956 and had no clue regarding continuing his higher education. His parents were not interested in sending him to Rairangpur as there was no bridge on the Kanhu River with apparently no communication. There used to be 3-4 feet height of mud and commuters would hold bicycles on their shoulders to cross the river. After discontinuation of education for one year, he was able to persuade his parents to allow him to study in Rairangpur Government High School. He lived in the student hostel and passed matriculation in 1961. Since the Rairangpur College was yet to be established, there was no place to study further in Bamanghaty. He returned to his village to be an assistant teacher in the same school where he studied. A few years later, the Government decided to provide grant-in-aid to the school and declared that all the schools which did not have trained teachers would be closed. He went to Baripada, district headquarter of Mayurbhanj district to complete his Certified Teacher (CT) programme from 1965-67. In 1967, he re-joined the school as the headmaster, a few months before Droupadi Tudu joined the school. In the 1969-70 academic year, Droupadi was studying in class

Bisweswar Mohanta, Former Head Master of Uparbeda M.E. school with his wife Sushila Mohanta, Dubulabeda village, Bamanghaty Subdivision of Mayurbhanj District

seven. Droupadi would discuss topics till all her doubts were cleared. The most important feature of the school was that it had a craft section which no other school in the vicinity had. Sukadeb Giri was the craft teacher. This encouraged a lot of students to take interest in craft. Droupadi was also fond of knitting, crafts and practiced these always along with her studies. She could make plates, and bowls out of Sal leaves, and brooms so well that people would be astonished at her craftsmanship.

Basant Giri, Former Teacher, Uparbeda U.P. School with his wife Pratibha Manjari Giri from Baliadhipa village, Bamanghaty Subdivision of Mayurbhanj District

On 22 February 1968, Jagabandhu Majhi left the job of the teacher as his home was far off. He was also from an affluent family and a practitioner of Homeopathy medicine. Then, the school committee decided to appoint Basudeb Behera as the assistant teacher when he was 16 years 5 months old, and had just passed his matriculation exam in first division from Rairangpur High School. During that time the District Inspector (DI) of schools, Goura Mohan Das and committee members would yield enormous power in the management of schools, especially in appointments of teachers. Basudeb worked in the school till 1974. He was an extremely industrious young man from neighbouring Tentoposi village who taught Droupadi for three months in class six and a full year in class seven. Basudeb Behera had also studied in the Uparbeda U.P. and M.E. school. He along with his classmates had organized Saraswati Pooja in the school under the guidance of the teachers in 1963 around the time when Droupadi started schooling. Later on, with his perseverance, he completed intermediate, Bachelor's, and a master's degree along with the Certification for Teachers (C.T.) and the bachelor's in education (B.Ed.) degrees. He lives in Tentoposi village with his wife Somalata, three daughters and one son all of whom are working at different places of the state now. He used to teach Mathematics and History to Droupadi's class. He also taught Sanskrit and Hindi during his tenure. Basu Sir (Basu Mastre), as he was fondly called, was a highly spirited teacher who led an exemplary life. He never consumed meat as a part of his principle of Jeeve daya (compassion to animals). He rendered free education by conducting additional tuition classes. These values got ingrained in the minds of the students.

He has been living in Tentoposi village for six generations since his great grandfather's father Pana Behera migrated from Dibadiha village of Chhotanagpur district of erstwhile Bihar (now Jharkhand) to Tentoposi village adjacent to Uparbeda in 1850. Being from the Kumbhar (potter) profession, the family enjoyed the patronage of the local Sarvarakars and Sardars as earthen pots and utensils were widely used in those times and the family catered to the needs of the villages around.

Her father would source old books for Droupadi as he could not purchase any book for Droupadi. Often these books would be torn. Droupadi would prepare gum made from hot rice and glue the torn portion for its durability. Sometimes, she would wonder why her father was not buying any new books for her. However, once in a while, if one new book could be purchased for her, she would be very happy. Droupadi was a very attentive listener and a student with a photographic memory. She would remember anything by listening to it only once. This made her a great favourite of all the teachers. The academic year, 1969-70 was eventful as that was the last year of Droupadi's schooling in the village.

A big dream was waiting to be born. In a class of 48 comprising eight girl students, Droupadi topped the merit list. There were no girl students who had secured first place since the school was established. Droupadi Tudu was also the youngest to secure the highest marks in the school. She was a repository of many virtues as she was sincere, compassionate, intelligent, and soft-spoken at the same time. She would address other students at the school as *Bhai* (brother), and *Nani* (sister) creating a family ambience in the school. She had neighbours having surnames as Giri and Mohanty etc. who spoke Odia in their households. All the children of Tudu, Giri and Mohanty households would play together and thus forged strong bonds as neighbours. This resulted in Droupadi learning to speak very fluent Odia along with her mother tongue Santali. The exposure to a multicultural community made her excel in the Odia medium education that she received in her school life.

Droupadi did not even have a pen while appearing for the scholarship examination. Her father brought some used pens from family and friends. These pens would not work long. However, she was happy with so many pens and often displayed them to her friends and family with a sense of abundance. She appeared for scholarship examinations in class-III, V, and VII. She did not even have a science notebook. Though sometimes, it would cross her mind that her father was not bringing books and pens for her, she did not allow that to be a deterrent to her learning. She would learn braving the odds and was able to answer all questions with her memory and intelligence. Droupadi used to be the top scorer in her class. During those days, the topper in the class would be made the class monitor. Droupadi asked Basudeb Sir if she could be a monitor. He agreed and she was made the monitor. She would command respect among her classmates. Teachers would entrust her the work of motivating students who were not sincere in studies. She used to take care of them diligently as well. Once, when Basudeb Sir was teaching Mathematics, he did not find a duster in the classroom. During that time, Basudeb Sir's grandfather passed away, so as customary, he had to shave his head. The bald headed Basudeb was wearing a cap. In the class with finding no alternative he took out his cap and wiped the blackboard with it to write further. This act of the teacher prompted laughter in the class, something which the observant Droupadi noticed. Next day, she appeared in the class with two handmade dusters made from old clothes and handed them over to Sir. The ability to take responsibility and display sensitivity for her surroundings was evident from her childhood.

Seeing her dedication, teachers would tell her father Biranchi that his daughter will pass the matriculation examination and will become a teacher. Droupadi also wanted to be a schoolteacher. Basudeb Sir once asked all the students about the aim of their lives. Many students expressed their goals, whereas some others blushed. However, a thoughtful Droupadi told her teacher that given an opportunity she wanted to become a teacher. The following chapters narrate her journey as a school teacher.

She was good at sports and took part in many intra-school competitions held to mark special occasions viz., Independence Day, Republic Day etc. She used to take part in running races (sprint), *Jhilpi* race, *Puchi* competition, Musical Chairs. Every time Droupadi would come first, and her best friend would come second. Once she purposefully ran slow to let her best friend Prabhati Giri to win. Later when asked by her teacher, she said that her friend will feel good to win and she felt glad to see her win at least once. Droupadi's magnanimity manifested even in later parts of her public life. Apart from Prabhati Abanti, Basanti, Pratibha, Bhagabati, Bharati, and Jamuna were the other friends she had. Droupadi was the youngest and the cutest among all.

During the recess of school, she used to tell stories of Ramayana and Mahabharat to her friends. How did young Droupadi learn all these stories staying in the village without access to a good library half a century before the internet era? Droupadi's father owned two precious books viz., Dandi Ramayan of Balaram Das and Mahabharat. While Droupadi was studying in class two, she used to read these books in the *Dhana Khala* (grain yard) which surprised many. Biranchi was very nonchalant about his daughter's unusual feat. He candidly said, since she could read Odia alphabets and is already in class two, she could read these sacred texts as well. However, all her teachers, kith and kin knew that it was something very extraordinary for the age.

There were many such stories about her life. One instance of bravery was when she swam through the turbulent stream on a heavily rainy day to attend class when none of the girl students turned up. Though she was not a regular swimmer, she beat all odds to reach school. It was during the rainy *Shravan* month in Hindu Calendar around Gamha (Rakhi Poornima) time in the month of August. Then, Droupadi was just 12-year-old. It surprised many as how could the young girl swim the stream with water approximately 3-4 feet deep? At that time, there was also an announcement that whosoever attends all the classes without fail would get an award at the end of the year. That was the motivation for this girl who wished to excel in academics, come what may.

Anand Chandra Giri was the president of the school while she was studying in class six. He was a gifted *Pala* singer. He used to teach *Pala* (an educational form of performing arts of Odisha) students every Saturday. Droupadi used to sing these songs. The poems of legendary poets, Prakriti Kabi Gangadhar Meher, Kabi Samrat Upendra Bhanj, Abhimanyu Samanta Singhara, Kabibar Radhanath Ray, Radhanath Rath etc. were taught in the school. Giri would sing these songs and to teach students as an extracurricular activity. He would sing these legendary Odia songs in his melodious voice in Odissi, Ramkeri, Bangalashree, Chokhi *Chhânda* (rhythm/meter).

One such patriotic song reverberated the vibrant rural school written by Bhakta Kabi Madhusudan Rao sung in Chokhi meter,

"Tu hi Maa janama Bhumi, Pabitra Bharata bhumi,
Tohari Santana Ambhe atu Sarabe.
Tora sricharana seba, pain mana prana deba,
gaiba tohari nama ananda rabe,
To anande hoiba khusi, kandiba dukhare tora hoina na dukhi."

All the teachers and students used to learn these songs. Droupadi had a mellifluous voice and she would sing during the school prayers. Even bystanders and people commuting in the road used to stop for some time to listen to her songs. It is a common notion that good education is available in cities. But it is commendable to note how a remote village of the country has enriched the lives of students and teachers in a holistic way by the efforts of committed and dedicated leaders.

She was deeply moved by Santha Kabi Bhima Bhois's couplets. Their meaning had an indelible impact on her. One of the most famous couplets, "*Praninka Arata Dukha Apramita Dekhu Dekhu keba Sahu. Mo Jeevana Pachhe Narke Padithau, Jagata Uddhara heu*". (The devotee says, there are a lot of miseries in the world and how the Lord tolerates witnessing those. Let my life rot in hell, if needed, but let the world be redeemed). Satha Kabi Bhima Bhoi (Ca 1855-1894) was a famous 19th century Gondh poet, saint, philosopher, influenced by Mahima Dharma. His Bhajans (devotional songs) and Bolis (a form of performing arts) are very popular in Odisha households. Nothing is known about his parents. The legend says that he was found lying on a lotus leaf in the pond by Dhaneswar Kondh and his wife. They brought him up. He was very poor and grazed cattle for his livelihood. He studied very little and started serving people. Eventually, he became a poet. Since he was blind and saintly, he was named as 'Andha Kabi' (visually impaired poet) and Santha Kabi (Saintly poet) in Odisha He was a great influence on Droupadi who learnt his songs during her time in the school.

Her uncle Banaju was a very good make-up artist who would dress up historical and mythological characters in village drama competitions and entertainment programmes. As a child, Droupadi loved and learnt the skills of dressing up different characters of history and mythology to perfection. Those days, music, dance, sports were also taught along with the academic subjects in the school as well. These added up to the holistic growth of students. During 1969-70, Nityananda Mohanta was the School Inspector (SI) in Kusumi Block. Since he was all alone as an academic administrator, he entrusted some of his responsibilities to two senior teachers of the block. These two teachers would inspect primary schools. One of the teachers was Prabhakar Nanda, Head Master, Hatbadla U.P.School. For 8-10 primary schools, there used to be a nodal school. The nodal school would organize a unique teaching pedagogy by a few senior teachers which was attended by teachers of all these 8-10 schools at regular intervals to enhance their teaching skills. However, the SI would not inspect the administration of Middle English schools during those days. The SI could only collect relevant data from M.E. Schools and send it to the government for the purpose of documentation.

Once, Prabhakar Nanda visited Uparbeda M.E.School. Everyone in the locality knew him and he was revered for his erudition and brilliance. He used to multi-task and was also working as a postmaster. He could treat patients by prescribing Homeopathy medicines as well. While returning after collecting data, he visited Uparbeda M.E. School. He asked the students to introduce themselves in class seven. When the turn of girl students came, they introduced themselves viz., Pratibha, Pratima, Abanti, Basanti, Bhagawati, Bharati, Droupadi etc. Most of the names signified great historical characters and were a treat to the ears. He knew Droupadi's father as well. He described the name of Droupadi

Tudu to the class saying the following things. "In Mahabharat, Droupadi depicts the quality of *Sarvamsaha* (resilient), the epitome of patience, perseverance, and valour. Tudu means 'To do'. You are here to do work for the upliftment of the society." These words of his were nothing short of a prophecy. It was laid into the hands of the mighty and powerful 'time' the job to prove it correct.

Once Basudeb Sir, wrote an impromptu Odia couplet on the wall just above the black board in class seven. It goes as follows:

> *"Dhana Nathile Kisa Hoiba, Manare achi Bala.*
> *Manara Bale Kari paremu Duniya talamala."*

(Even though there is a lack of resources, I have the mental strength to move the world.)

He used to draw pictures and encourage students to give wings to their imagination. He was very dedicated to the education and welfare of his village. He was also deeply involved in the social life of the area and contributed his fullest to its growth. The Santhals have a custom of naming the grandchildren after their grandparent's name as they believe that the blessings come through the ancestors. They also believe in re-births of a soul and very likely, the deceased grandparents take birth in the same family as the grandchildren. It is said that some souls have choices, and some do not.

A dozen students in the same class were named Bhagat, leading to confusion among teachers. Once during a *Vidyarambha* ceremony, during *Saraswati Pooja*, Basudeb Behera slightly altered their names with the consent of their parents to lessen the confusion while teaching in a class. So, the many children whose names were Bhagat were slightly modified to Bhagawat, Bhagirath, Bhakta bandhu etc.

All the children would take part in the festivals and celebrations in the village irrespective of their faith, signifying harmony in diversity. While Tapati would attend *Sarool Pooja, a Santhal festival* in *Jaher Garh* where the divine was offered flowers of Sal

Tree (*Sargi Phula*), Droupadi would attend *Shiva Ratri* in *Sindhukeswar* Temple and become a worshiper of Lord Shiva. The Divine consciousness always made her stand tall and lead a path forward. Droupadi and her friends would wear new clothes whenever possible. Alternatively, they would wash the clothes made on the last festival and wear them with elan. Those days, there would be one or two dresses for the children in most of the households. Since Droupadi's mother did not know stitching, Droupadi could not have her clothes repaired even if the clothes were torn. She would use safety pins and wear the clothes with multiple holes. Droupadi would sometimes ask her father to bring a new dress for her. Her father would say, when he would visit Rairangpur and he would buy a good dress for her and that he did not want to purchase ordinary dresses for his daughter from the weekly haat. Droupadi would be happy with these statements. In reality, Biranchi did not have adequate resources to purchase clothes for his daughter. Nevertheless, there was abundance in their consciousness. The focus was more on community celebration and happiness and less on personal adornments. Maybe they knew in their hearts that all paths led to the same God. Droupadi would sing songs and teach her juniors about lessons of human values. During those days, she would partake of non-vegetarian food which her family would prepare.

Once, when she was studying in class five, Droupadi's grand-mother had purchased a *Pauja* (anklets) by paying Rs. 20/- from a jewellery shop for her granddaughter. A joyful Droupadi walked everywhere with her anklets making a tinkling sound in the courtyard, neighbourhood and all the possible places. When Biranchi Narayan returned home, he asked about the anklets and said, "I do not want to decorate my daughter externally. I would like her to possess a beautiful mind and golden heart. These external accessories are not necessary for her". Listening to the words of the strict Biranchi Narayan, Droupadi removed the anklets and handed them over to her mother. Later, she came to know that those were returned to the shop the next day. Droupadi was saddened by this act. She felt that her father was not buying anything for her. Biranchi would say, when he would be capable enough to possess more wealth, he would buy gold ornaments for her.

Another such incident happened soon after. Droupadi's stepmother was quite well off and was staying with her father, as she did not have any brothers to take care of her parents. So, she and her sisters were looking after them. Her father had landed properties and had a decent living. There would be weekly *haats* (fairs), in Mayurbhanj where every household would purchase food materials, clothes and many essential items and store them for the whole week. Once on a *haat* day, Droupadi saw her stepmother going to the fair. Both exchanged pleasantries and she asked Droupadi to accompany her to the *haat*. The innocent young Droupadi was excited and agreed on a condition that she should be gifted a particular saree. The deal was sealed, and both went together to the *haat*. Droupadi was given the saree of her choice and she came back joyfully with the precious possession. She was extremely jubilant and showed the saree to everyone. In the evening, when Biranchi Narayan returned home, he came to know about it, and he went into a fit of terrible rage. In his anger, he hit Droupadi mercilessly till blood oozed out from her back. Droupadi was in utter bewilderment. She was deeply hurt, and felt sad that her father did not let her possess anything new. However, years later she could understand the meaning of his behaviour and learnt to live in austerity. Droupadi grew up under strict supervision of her father to evolve as a self-made and independent personality.

In 2000, the Uparbeda Upper Primary and Middle English school which existed separately and at a distance of one kilometre from each other were merged to one school in the premises of Uparbeda Upper Primary school imparting education from class one to class eight. Named Sarakari Uchha Prathamika Vidyalaya, Uparbeda the school carrying a rich legacy is as picturesque as it used to be. The Department of School and Mass Education, Government of Odisha imparts free education to all the students.

Chankaya has said in the court of Dhananaanda, "*Shikshak Sadharan nahin hota. Sristi aur Pralaya uske godi main khilte hai* "(A teacher is not ordinary. He is the reason for construction and destruction). True to these words, even in the remotest part of the village few dedicated teachers and parents shaped the formative years of young Droupadi which find reflection throughout her life. The Uparbeda upbringing and education were pivotal to her personality, and she upheld those values in her life.

Chapter - 3

Elevation through Education (1970-79)

Droupadi completed her class seven from Uparbeda Middle English. School. She secured the highest marks among 48 students. She wanted to continue studying further but did not know how to progress.

Her *Bada bapa* (uncle) from the Sardar lineage, Karthik Chandra Majhi had won the election and became a Member of the Legislative Assembly of Rairangpur in 1967 as a Swatantra Party candidate from Rairangpur constituency. He was the Minister in the fourth Assembly of Odisha under the chief ministership of Rajendra Narayan Singhdeo. He had held various portfolios during the span of four years, viz., Finance, Home (Public Health Engineering of the R. & B. Branch), Urban Development, Works, Transport, Tribal & Rural Welfare.

After the completion of class seven, Droupadi along with her father Biranchi Narayan met the minister Majhi. Droupadi showed him all her certificates and expressed her interest in going for higher studies. Mr Majhi was very pleased to see her interest in higher education. He instructed an officer to help her out. Those days, caste certificates had to be procured from the district headquarter, Baripada which was more than 80 kilometres from her village. It was very difficult for her to procure it. The minister's aide helped her in getting the required caste certificate, which was a prerequisite for her higher studies. Droupadi eventually, applied to this scheme.

In those days, students from scheduled castes and scheduled tribes could avail free residential education from government schools. One had to apply to the Tribal & Rural Welfare (now ST & SC development, Minorities and Backward classes welfare) department of the state. There were student quotas from thirteen (now thirty) districts of Odisha. From the prescribed castes, a certain number of students were chosen based on merit to study in the special residential government schools. The population of scheduled castes and scheduled tribes was approximately 40 percent of the total population of the state. The government schemes eventually did multiply over the subsequent years. However, the awareness of such schemes and policies among the beneficiaries steadily rose with passage of time, due to the IEC (Information, Education and Communication) activities of the Government. It was not very easy for her to take advantage of such schemes owing to the lack of awareness of this information.

One day, a postcard arrived carrying the news of her selection. Droupadi's joy knew no bounds. Her parents and extended family were also extremely happy as she would be the first girl from Uparbeda village to travel to the state capital, Bhubaneswar which was approximately 280 kilometres away, to pursue higher education.

She packed all her essentials in a tin trunk and started for Bhubaneswar via Keonjhar. There was no direct road or rail transport available from Rairangpur to Bhubaneswar in those days. She had to travel to Keonjhar and stay in a distant relative's place. After searching for quite some time, they reached the relative's place. They had packed rice and vegetables for their use during the stay, as they did not wish to be a burden to their hosts. Such was Biranchi Narayan's self- respect and sense of responsibility. They stayed at the relative's place that night. Next morning, they boarded a bus to Bhubaneswar from Keonjhar. They could have travelled enroute the Mayurbhanj district headquarter Baripada.

However, since they did not have any acquaintances in Baripada, Biranchi Narayan did not find it prudent to travel with his daughter on a route where they may have to make a night halt at the railway station or the bus stand. Finally, they reached Bhubaneswar. Biranchi was carrying Droupadi's big tin box. Droupadi had never seen her father holding such a big piece of luggage. Being the headman of the village, people around him would always be there to assist. However, he did not mind lifting heavy luggage belonging to his daughter. They hired a rickshaw and after some time, reached the residence of Minister Kartik Chandra Majhi. They had reached their destination after travelling for two full days,

The story of Droupadi's admission in the school is also interesting and hilarious. On reaching the Unit 2 Girls High School, the teacher in charge of admissions asked her, her name. All the teachers in the school were talking in chaste Odia. Droupadi and some other girls from Mayurbhanj were used to speaking Odia in a different dialect. Though she was fluent in writing the Odia language, she found it difficult to communicate orally. On the day of her admission, perhaps she was also very nervous.

Tuma Naa Kana? (What is your name?). She could not figure out what was being asked. 'Uparbeda', she replied. On hearing that, the class laughed. Then she asked *Tuma Gaon naa?* (What is the name of your village?), to this she replied: "Droupadi Tudu" There was more laughter. Understanding the challenge that the new student was facing, the teacher modified the conversation and asked gently, '*Tuma Naama Kana*'? (What is your name?). Now Droupadi could understand and replied, Droupadi Tudu. However, her friends Chuni and Kuni called her Uparbeda for quite some time to keep the joke alive in the class. Soon she had learnt to enjoy the joke too.

In July of 1970, Droupadi took admission in class eight in the Unit 2 Girls' High School which had approximately 1200 girl students. A room was allotted to her in a designated hostel known as the 'Special Hostel for SC, ST students' (now Kuntala Kumari Sabat Adivasi Girls' Hostel), which housed nearly 100 girls belonging to the scheduled tribe. All ST, SC students who got admission in the school had the opportunity to avail of the hostel facilities. Droupadi thus got a new address, a new identity, and wings to fly and conquer the world. Once the formalities for her admission in the school were completed, her father returned to the village.

In those times, relatively few districts of Odisha sent students to study in schools and live in hostels, a number very low in comparison to their quota (It is part of an affirmative action towards inclusion of the diverse minority communities in India). So, the students of other districts in the waiting list were given an opportunity. Dangi Murmu, another tribal girl from Purunapani village, near Manada and Bisoi of Mayurbhanj district got the opportunity to take admission in the second selection as some seats were vacant. She got her selection letter in August 1970. Daughter of an eminent Adivasi leader Bhagabat Murmu and the third child in a family of six sisters, she joined the school a month after Droupadi. Droupadi and Dangi were from the same district and same subdivision and struck a bond which would continue for a lifetime. Tribal girls from almost all districts of Odisha would come there for studies. It was a big exposure for Droupadi and Dangi. Other prominent districts of the state were Keonjhar, Sundergarh, Koraput, Kandhamal, Dhenkanal, and Balasore. Students from various tribes viz., Kondh, Santhal, Ho, Bhumia, Gond, Munda, and Oram also took admission in the school. They enriched the campus life by displaying their traditions and values, all of which was invaluable learning for Droupadi. She was witnessing a mini-Odisha inside her campus and was learning from every one of them. Initially, when the students joined the school, the teachers in school would take them for exposure visits - for *darshan* of Lord Sri Jagannath temple in Puri, the Sun temple in Konark, the caves of Khandagiri and Udayagiri, and the Shiva temple in

Kapilash, Dhenkanal. These visits in her formative years enriched her immensely.

The students would observe every festival in the school. Saraswati Pooja, Ganesh Pooja, Kumar Poornima, Makar Sankranti, Deepavali, Rath Yatra, Durga Pooja to name a few, with dance, music, rangoli and food. All the tribal girls would eat together, play together, and would have a lot of merrymaking to mark every festival.

Shantilata Gachhayat, a motherly and caring hostel superintendent would monitor the welfare of the girls and encourage them to live in camaraderie in a hostel full of cultural diversity. She would encourage the girls to celebrate the festivals of all districts since they were coming from various parts of the state. That is how a student of Mayurbhanj got to know about the culture of Koraput, Sundergarh and vice versa. During Saraswati Pooja and Ganesh Pooja, the students would do *Chuda ghasa*. The cuisine is prepared by grinding beaten rice flakes and mixing them with sugar and coconut. Other delicious cuisines viz., *Chhole* (curry made of chickpeas), *Puri (deep-fried whole wheat bread), Bundia (sweet balls made of gram flour), Seo (Bhujia)* would be prepared by the hostel cook. The school had a lovely garden with all types of flowers. They would pluck flowers and make beautiful garlands for the deities. The priest would come in the morning to perform *Pooja* (worshipping), offer *Pushpanjali* (offering of flowers), and break a coconut as per the prevailing customs. After completion of the pooja by the priest, they would feast on the *Prasad* (food offering to the divine) together. The school and hostel were inside the same premise separated by a small gate.

During the Ganesh Pooja and Saraswati Pooja, the students in the school would dress up in new clothes. Droupadi had never purchased any dress material that cost more than Rs 5/- per metre. Her friend Chudamani stitched those dresses for her while she was in the Unit-2 Girls High school.

Shantilata's twin daughters Chinmayee (Chuni) and Tanmayee (Kuni) were also her classmates. Chuni and Droupadi were great friends as Chuni was very bubbly and talkative. The mother and twin daughters would also stay in the hostel premise in the superintendent quarter while her husband and sons would stay outside in the official quarters as men were not allowed in the girl's hostel. Most of the students were day scholars.

Chuni and Kuni would take part in the Scouts and Guides. Chuni recollects that, she along with a few of her friends would grab pickles and Ambula (sour dried mangoes) secretly and eat in a quiet place. Chuni lived in a household of five siblings and parents who were freedom fighters. Shantilata and her husband Gandharba Gachhayat served the nation in different capacities with utmost loyalty. After India attained political independence, Gandharba Gachhayat opted to take up the responsibility of Head Master of Sunabeda High School which was 500 kilometres away from his home town Bhubaneswar.

Droupadi Tudu with school friends Dangi Murmu & Sumitra Kisku in Unit-2 Girls High School, Bhubaneswar, Odisha in class XII, 1974

Droupadi's twin friends, Chinmayee (Chuni) & Tanmayee (Kuni) with their mother Shantilata Gachhayat, Superintendent of Special Hostel for SC, ST students (now Kuntala Kumari Sabat Adivasi Girls' Hostel) Unit 2 Girls High School, Bhubaneswar

Droupadi's room mate & best friend Dangi Murmu from Special Hostel for SC, ST students' (now Kuntala Kumari Sabat Adivasi Girls' Hostel) Unit 2 Girls High School, Bhubaneswar

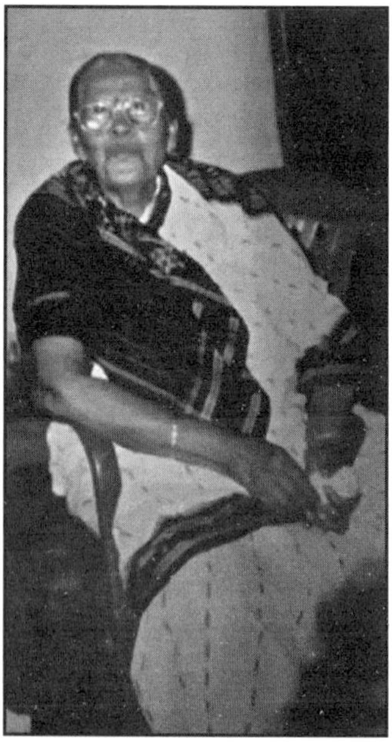

Shantilata Gachhayat, Hostel Superintendent, Kuntala Kumari Sabat Adivasi Girls' Hostel, Unit 2 Girls High School, Bhubaneswar

Droupadi excelled in both academics and sports. Her only focus was to study well and find a government job to help her father financially. She took part in shot put, javelin throw, and the discus throw in the school and later in the college sports competitions along with the National Cadet Corps (hereafter, NCC) classes.

To maintain discipline, Shantilata would read every post card the students would write to their families. Postcards were the only medium to send letters to near and dear ones those days. The inland letters and stamped envelopes were not allowed for students. Similarly, any letter received for the students would be scrutinised by her before being delivered to the students to maintain discipline in the hostel.

Once, after joining the Unit-2 Girls High School in class eight, Droupadi had written a letter to her father asking him to send Rs. 10/- by money order. As part of regular practice, Shantilata read the letter before posting it. She advised Droupadi against it saying that the government of Odisha was taking care of her stay, education and food and that she should not ask her father for any money. As an obedient adolescent, Droupadi made the necessary corrections in her letter immediately.

Droupadi would never gossip or waste time in her school and hostel. She never complained of her struggle as she knew these challenges would bring out the best in her. Often the teachers would cite example of the hard-working hostel girls to the day scholar students in the prayer classes. They were staying without any direct supervision of their parents whereas the day-scholar students were guided by their parents and family. Being out of home did not hinder the hostel girls' growth in any way.

The teachers in the girls' school were all ladies except two Sanskrit teachers (known as Pundits). Renuka Acharya would teach the first language Odia. "Gayatri Das taught second language English and was extremely talented. She would take extra care of the students especially those from Mayurbhanj as her brother

Nirmal Das was a Tehsildar (districts were divided into tehsils each having a revenue officer known as tehsildar) in Rairangpur." Dangi recollects, "Gayatri Das's husband was also an accomplished writer. She introduced the students to the literary world. The school was like a caring family. Basudeb Acharya was a Sanskrit Pandit. Another teacher was Sandhyarani Dey. One teacher would teach multiple subjects in those days.

There were so many activities in the school that the students had no time to feel home sick. Droupadi would play the character of male protagonist in the school drama and act brilliantly. Along with Dangi she also participated in NCC under the guidance of their teacher Kanakabala Mohanty. Dangi recalled that she could not make it to an out station NCC camp as she was unable to arrange Rs. 60/- needed for the camp. However, these financial challenges did not dampen their morale. They would never hanker after riches and opulence. Droupadi would not even ask for her refreshment food packet distributed in the NCC camp. Often it was Dangi who would secure her packet for her.

Many resident students would have one or two good dresses to wear to school which they had brought from home. The school would provide free education, accommodation, and books. They would wash the clothes in the evening and dry them in a manner that they could use them on the next day. They would use the bathing soap to clean the clothes, so that the dresses would smell good.

Suchitra Samal, another scholar whose home was near the school, was the monitor of the class. Droupadi and other students cooperated well with her. She continued to organize alumni get-togethers of the batch mates in the years to come. In Uparbeda, Droupadi had been the monitor. She used to lead the team. However, she had the ability to lead as well as follow with equal ease. Though Suchitra was well off, she also managed with 4-5 pairs of dresses. When asked about the same, Suchitra Samal says,

"The times and society were such that it did not believe in hoarding clothes." Maybe it was because the society practised *Aparigraha* (the virtue of non-hoarding). Those days, there used to be a thin line between the haves and have-nots. The students would be friends irrespective of their family background and everyone would wear uniforms to school.

The students in the hostel would mostly stay in the premises. If they needed to go out to buy something, the girls would be escorted by one of the hostel staff. Shantilata would keep a note of all this. She would ask the girls to keep the windows open so that she could monitor them, and students could focus on studies in a better way. She would look after the students like a mother if anyone was unwell. Apart from studies, cultural events and sports, the students also learned knitting, embroidery, painting, gardening, and vocational skills.

The bonding between the senior and the junior students was very strong. The juniors adored their seniors. They would never talk in loud voices, nor would they ever be discourteous with their seniors. The school campus was student driven. There would be students in-charge of all verticals at the school. For example, a *Khadya Manti* (Minister of food) was responsible for managing the mess. She would prepare the menu and procure the ingredients with the help of the mess staff. She would monitor the quality of food. Similarly, '*Samay Manti*' (Minister of punctuality) was responsible for time management and discipline of students. She would ring the bell for the waking up, prayer, meals time, sleeping time etc. This culture helped in shaping the personality of students for generations. Dangi had Physiology Hygiene as the optional in matriculation examination. "During those days, there would be no one to career counsel the students. We would take whatever subjects our friends would choose. Someone advised this as an easier option. So, I opted for it," Dangi recounted.

Droupadi would come home once a year during summer vacation. Shantilata *didi* would give bus fare to all students. She would give the exact fare for each girl by name individually, based on the distance from Bhubaneswar to their respective homes. The bus fare used to be very nominal. The fare for Bhubaneswar to Baripada bus was Rs. 8/- only. She would board the Government bus of Odisha Road Transport (now Odisha State Road Transport Corporation) in Bhubaneswar in the evening and reach Baripada early morning on the next day. Then she would take another bus from Baripada to Rairangpur. Later on, a private night bus started plying from Bhubaneswar to Rairangpur. She would board the bus near her school hostel at Unit 2 in Bhubaneswar. The red coloured bus would start in the morning from Baripada and would reach Rairangpur in three hours covering a distance of 86 kilometres approximately. She would get down at Kaduani Chhak bus stop a few miles ahead of Rairangpur and walk down 7 kilometres to reach her village Uparbeda. The Kanhu River is full in the rainy season and muddy for the rest of the year. However, she did not consider this as an obstacle but a challenge. The zest and zeal that this young girl had to progress and evolve was unmatched. When she was visiting her village, she would witness many girls from her school days getting married. They had not got an opportunity to study further. This would disturb her. She would say to her family that she would work to build a bridge on the Kanhu River. This was appreciated by her family even though they did not have any clue as to how this could be accomplished by the little girl. Her younger brother Bhagat (Pata) would always be delighted to see her back home. She would advise him to study well and help them in his studies.

Soon, it was time for their matriculation examination Students would have to study for long hours. Droupadi and a few of her friends would feel hungry in the afternoon. They would request the matron of the hostel to store the *peja* (the supernatant starchy liquid on the boiled rice.) They would have it, with lemon, chilli, and salt. There would be a rule in the hostel that, if any student observed fasting, the amount that would have been spent for the

Suchitra Samal, Droupadi Murmu's school friend & class monitor, Unit 2 Girls High School, Bhubaneswar

meal, would be paid to the student as stipend. Droupadi would fast for a few days a month to save some money which she could use for buying essentials.

Four years down the line, school life was over. It concluded with enormous learning and personality development. Droupadi consistently upskilled herself in every possible way. She was no longer confined to the wisdom gained in her village. She had new dreams for higher studies. There would be a group photograph every year for the senior batch prior to matriculation examination. In the eleventh class, which is the last year of her school career, she along with Sumitra Kisku and Dangi Murmu had clicked a black and white photograph, first ever with her school friends. The three girls were close friends and they wished to capture the moment as a fond memory. She returned to her hometown after appearing for the matriculation board examination. She passed the matriculation examination under the Board of Secondary Education, Orissa in 1974. She was the first girl of her village to pass the matriculation examination. Her joy knew no bounds and the family was euphoric. Her father had always wished his daughter to be well- educated, and she had just fulfilled his first dream.

After passing matriculation, she decided to continue her studies. This was a big dream for her and her family. She had to collect her school leaving certificate, conduct certificate, and mark sheet from the school. It took quite some time for this. By the time, all the documents could be procured, the last date of admission college was over. She could not take admission in college for the intermediate programme in the 1974-75 academic session.

In 1975, an important political event happened in the town in which Droupadi's teacher from Uparbeda recollected, "Biranchi Narayan Tudu, and a group of friends walked almost 20 kilometres on 22 January 1975 to attend a political meeting conducted by the then Prime Minister, Indira Gandhi at the Bikash Nagar ground in Rairangpur. This was a few months ahead of the proclamation of internal emergency. Lakhs of people gathered to have a glimpse of the charismatic leader as she landed in a chopper at 9.30 AM. She spoke for two minutes in Santali, one minute in Odia and the rest of her speech was delivered in Hindi. People were amazed at her language skills. The MLA of Rairangpur had contributed the Odia and Santali portion for her speech."

Droupadi's teacher was also a part of the Uparbeda group though he was working in Nagbhan U.P.School those days. Biranchi Narayan was mesmerised and told that since she was the daughter of the Prime Minister Jawaharlal Nehru, she could be so talented and was flying in the sky. Would this be possible for any woman in his household? Never did he imagine what was in store for his own daughter.

Droupadi could have taken admission in Rairangpur College but commuting from her village to the College would be difficult on a daily basis. She could not afford to stay in private hostels. She discontinued her studies that year and stayed in Uparbeda. She applied for Rama Devi Women's College (Now Rama Devi Women's University) for the 1975-76 academic year and secured a seat in Intermediate of Arts. She passed Intermediate in 1977 and took admission in Bachelor of Arts programme with Political Science and Economics as her main subjects. Those days, Rama Devi Women's College was affiliated to Utkal University. She was staying in the Adivasi Women's hostel (now known as Indira Gandhi Post-Matric Adivasi Women's Hostel or IGST) which offered free accommodation for scheduled tribe girls from the scheduled tribes. Brajeswari Mishra was the hostel superintendent and was very popular among students.

Sanjukta Majhi, daughter of Kartik Chandra Majhi and her cousin reminisced that Droupadi was very studious. "Our grand-fathers were brothers, and we were from the same village. Droupadi didi was 4-5 years elder to us. However, I lived in Bhubaneswar with my parents. Later on, I was working with the Department of Women and Child welfare, Government of Odisha. I joined the state government service as the supervisor of Integrated Child Development Scheme (ICDS) promoted later to Child Development Project Officer (CDPO). I took voluntary retirement when I was serving as the Programme Officer. I worked in various districts including Cuttack, Khurda, Puri, and Mayurbhanj."

Delha Majhi (now Delha Soren), another girl from Dalki village in the Kusumi block of Mayurbhanj district, was two years senior

Delha Soren, Droupadi Murmu's senior in Ramadevi College, Bhubaneswar

to Droupadi. She had also joined Rama Devi Women's college as an intermediate student of Arts. The Adivasi Women's hostel was not built then. So, she was staying in the special Hostel for SC, ST students in Unit 2 Girls' High School where Droupadi was staying. She would commute from Unit 2 to Rama Devi college every day in a city bus by paying just 10 paisa. Those days, very few students from Mayurbhanj would go for studies in the capital city. Droupadi and Delha bonded well and would travel together while returning home.

Biranchi Narayan would send money orders of Rs. 10/- a month to Droupadi while she was in the college. Droupadi was also getting a stipend. The money was sufficient for her as they neither went out to eat nor did they have any other expenses apart from buying oil, soap and some necessary items required in the hostel. Droupadi never watched movies as she did not have much money. She would say, she did not like watching movies. She never ate out at a restaurant with any friend as she could not have repaid the favour. She would have whatever the mess would offer. However, Droupadi and Delha would sneak out from their busy daily routine once in a while to have few *Golgappas/Gupchup* near their college. Each *Golgappa* would cost as little as 10 paise and a plate of *chaat* would cost 50 paise then. Delha took care of Droupadi like an elder sister.

Droupadi and Delha would spend time practising dancing, singing and acting after study hours. Gobinda Soren would teach them acting. Droupadi would play the male protagonist (hero) and would look very handsome in a male attire. She was tall and was she excellent in acting. Once, a series of plays were enacted for a period of one week by the Mahila Samiti. These plays were inspired by a legendary leader of Odisha. One of the famous plays named *Kardheni Jeni Manyapam* (Karma connects hearts), had a beautiful Santali romantic song enacted by Droupadi Tudu as the hero and another friend Parbati Kisku as the heroine (female protagonist).

"Einaah monay, doo gaatay, baha raynah soo.
Aamaah monay, doo gaate, jeal jhaarna.
Buru lodom, bir baha, baha bhusal en.
Gota pala, sondhal soo doo, otaang seter en.
Koel raahaa, teenj, gol aam, naasay aanjom may.
Paantay, paantay, naapaam aalang, buru lodom re.
Einaah monay, doo gaatay, baha raynah soo."
Aamaah monay, doo gaate jeal jhaarna.

(My mind is like a fragrant flower. Your mind is like a natural spring. We are meeting in the plains of the jungle. I shall blow a whistle in the tone of a nightingale. You may please give it a hearing. Our union pervades all over like the fragrance of a flower that blossomed in the forest.)

She would address Delha as Muni didi fondly. Once she told her, "My father had a small shop and would give me one rupee every day. I would return the money as I had nothing to buy. I wish I had kept that money which would be a big amount now.' Both would laugh at this. Delha passed the Bachelor of Arts with History and Political Science as subjects in 1977. She was also preparing to appear for the examination for a government job.

Droupadi owned only one or two sarees. She would starch the sarees on Sundays with rice water and dry them straight to be used for the upcoming six days of the week. Every day after coming back from college, she would fold the saree properly and put it under the pillow or bed to remove the wrinkles. Even though she had a few sarees, she would be neatly dressed all the time.

The student union elections used to be a very important event in the college. This was more interesting for a women's college like Rama Devi, as every candidate would put her best effort to win. Saroj Nalini Parida, Droupadi's batchmate won the election as the president of the college union for the academic year 1978-79 with many votes received from students of Adivasi Women's hostel. Similarly, the posts of Vice President, Secretary, Joint

Secretary, Dramatic Secretary, Sports Secretary etc. would be elected by the students. A time between 10 AM and 4 PM would be fixed for students to cast their vote. One day before the election, the students would deliver the popular speech of the campus to defend their stand. This would be attended by all the students. The festivities and zeal of the students would be unparalleled. This practice introduced students to the values of democracy. Often, political parties would support various candidates and fund the event too.

Delha worked for six months on contract in the Tribal & Rural Welfare department of Government of Odisha as one of the existing employees was on leave. She then qualified the special examination of accountant held in 1979, which selected more than 60 students. She started working in the Accountant General Office of Bhubaneswar as an accountant and continued there till her retirement. She stayed in the college hostel for a few months and then applied for the quarters. In a span of two months, she was allotted a quarter in Unit 4 A.G. Colony of Bhubaneswar. Droupadi graduated from Rama Devi Women's College with Bachelor of Arts with Political Science and Economics as her subjects, in 1979. She became the first girl from the village to earn a degree, bringing glory to her family.

On the home front, Droupadi witnessed the birth of her youngest brother Taranisen Tudu (Diku) on 5 March 1977. He was the third and youngest child of Biranchi Narayan and Singo. Being the youngest child, he was pampered in the household. Droupadi would also take care of him. He was more interested in sports and making friends in the village like many other children of his age in the Uparbeda.

During college days, she would avail of the Government bus plying from Bhubaneswar to Rairangpur and would board the bus from the Vani Vihar bus stop in Bhubaneswar and get down in Kaduani Chhak as usual. From Kaduani, she would again walk seven kilometres to reach her village Uparbeda enroute Kanhu

River. As mentioned, Kanhu River did not have any bridge then. She had to cross through the river holding her luggage. Once while coming in the bus, she met a young man who was also studying in Bhubaneswar and hailed from the same block as hers. He was Shyama Charan Murmu from Pahadpur village of Kusumi block of Mayurbhanj. Both became friends and would often travel together to their respective homes together. Gradually, their bond became stronger as they helped each other grow in life.

One of Droupadi's school friends from a different section was Archita Patnaik. She was one of the brightest among her classmates and was a day boarder as her family resided in Bhubaneswar. Later in life, she worked as a Professor in Chemistry in IIT Madras. Prof. Archita described Droupadi as a yogi. She admits it was beyond her imagination that a docile, young, quiet and under-privileged girl could ascend to be the first citizen of the country. Needless to say, she felt extremely proud of her.

Her formal education may have been over, but Droupadi kept upskilling herself and working on herself every passing day and did not leave any opportunities to gain knowledge from all aspects of life. Oblivious of the future opportunities, her preparation to Better herself continued.

Pradipta Kishore Das, Minister of Education, Government of Odisha lighting ceremonial lamp as the chief guest in the Annual day programme of Rama Devi College with the president of student

Pradipta Kishore Das, Minister of Education, Government of Odisha, Prof. Rama Sundari Devi was adviser to the student union, Saroj Nalini Parida, President, Student union Rama Devi College, Bhubaneswar in 1978

Chapter - 4

Money, Marriage, and Motherhood 1979-83

Droupadi could study up to a bachelor's degree from the prestigious Rama Devi Women's College of Utkal University. She decided to work soon after. By virtue of being from the tribal dominated Mayurbhanj district, she knew a few other tribal political leaders of the time from indirect sources. Staying in the capital city of the state for more than eight years had also broadened her vision. She could gather the necessary information and knowledge which would lead her to a decent government job.

The nieces of Saharai Oram, Minister, Rural Development were her classmates, and she would often visit their home walking from her hostel as she would not have the 25 paisa to spend on rickshaw fare. Oram had encouraged her to be self- sufficient and guided her as and when necessary. There, she came to know that she had to register her name in the employment exchange to get a call for a job interview. Oram also helped her to register her name in the employment exchange, Bhubaneswar to get a call for a job.

Soon, she got an interview call for the post of Junior Assistant. A massive interview of 300 vacancies had taken place for scheduled caste and scheduled tribe candidates. The selection was based on an interview. By her sincere endeavours, Droupadi qualified for the post of Junior Assistant, Department of Irrigation, Secretariat, Government of Odisha in 1979 at the age of 21, even before her final result of the bachelor's degree was declared. Later on, she worked in the Department of Power as well. She stayed with Delha

Majhi, her senior, who was working in the office of the Accountant General, Odisha in the quarters of the AG Colony, Unit 4 in Bhubaneswar. Delha was not married then. Droupadi approached Delha and expressed her desire to share accommodation with her to which Delha gladly agreed. In Delha Majhi's quarter, Gayamani Murmu (now Besra), Nina Kujur, and Droupadi Tudu stayed together. All the four girls were extremely committed to their work and family. Often Droupadi's younger brother Diku and father Biranchi Narayan would visit her in Bhubaneswar and stay with her.

Droupadi's younger brother Tarinisen Tudu (Diku)

Young Droupadi with her relative

Though Droupadi drew a modest salary, being financially independent was an immense joy and satisfaction to her. Droupadi was very hard working and possessed outstanding culinary skills too. She would go with Delha to buy vegetables and other essentials for the household. She would buy clothes and other household necessities for her family and send those to Uparbeda. Her parents would be thrilled to get gifts from their beloved daughter.

Her best friend, Dangi also joined the job on 16 April 1979 in Central Excise, Customs and Service Tax (now GST, Central Excise and Customs), Bhubaneswar zone under the Central Board of Indirect Taxes & Customs, Ministry of Finance, Government of India. They would often meet. They would have a get-together among the Adivasi students. The political leaders belonging to Mayurbhanj were acquaintances and relatives of many of them. Dangi's father Bhagawat Murmu was a friend of many prominent Adivasi leaders like Chandra Mohan Majhi, Arjun Majhi, and Chaitanya Prasad Majhi, to name a few.

Shyam Charan Murmu from the Pahadpur village of Badampahar, Mayurbhanj, Odisha was studying in the Buxi Jagabandhu Bidyadhar College, Bhubaneswar during that time. He was an accomplished soccer player and was the first student to pass the bachelor's degree from his village. As both belonged to the same nativity and were residing in Bhubaneswar for studies and to pursue a professional career, they would help each other in many ways. They used to meet often to discuss their careers. Shyam Charan would visit the office of the Accountant General in Bhubaneswar to meet Delha didi whom he would respect a lot. Shyam was working at Puri in the office of Deputy Accountant General. He was also appearing for a banking examination because he wanted to switch his job. He was a good student. He qualified the probationary examinations of seven banks in one year including Bank of Baroda, Union Bank and Bank of India etc. However, he preferred Bank of India as it was the leading bank in the

Mayurbhanj district, and he could stay close to his parental home. He was appointed as the probationary officer in the Bank of India.

Droupadi and Shyam had known each other for 3-4 years by then. Soon, they decided to become life partners and conveyed their proposal of marriage to their respective parents through the elders of the village in May 1980. According to the prevailing social customs, Santhal grooms are required to pay *pana* (bride's money) to the bride's family which is finalized before the marriage. Droupadi's father Biranchi Narayan Tudu did not wish his daughter to get married so soon. Droupadi had also joined a government post recently. However, Shyam Charan, determined to marry her, camped in the Uparbeda village in a relative's place along with two of his uncles and two other respectable persons of the village. In their presence the bride's money was finalized. It was one cow, one bull, 16 pairs of *Jhela* sarees (female clothing), 16 pairs of *Dhoti* (male clothing). According to Santhal traditions, if both parents of the bride are alive then the groom must give one cow and one bull in *pana* (bride's money). If only the mother is alive, then only the cow is to be given. Shyam's tenacity compelled Biranchi Narayan to consent for the marriage even though he was reluctant initially.

There are twelve types of marriages in Santhal traditions namely, *Sanga Bapla, Kadam Bapla, Kirin Bapla, Upagir Bapla, Tunki Dipil Bapla, Itut Bapla, Nirbelok Bapla, Diku Bapla, Sange Bariyat, Haram Bariiyat, Gardi Jawain.* These nomenclatures have been prescribed according to the rituals for each one. In the marriage a special saree has to be woven for the mother of the bride as a mark of respect. It would have to be 24 haat (12 yards). If the grandmother is alive, her saree has to be a bit longer, at least 25 *haat*. The aunts of the bride and her friends who accompany her to her in-laws would return wearing new clothes offered to them from the groom's family. The groom's family also provides rice and meat for the marriage feast for the village, to be organised by the bride's side. This ritual is known as *chedi*.

Droupadi and Shyam's marriage fell in the category of *Haram Bariiyat*. In this type of marriage, the groom after agreeing to pay the bride's money goes to the bride's place accompanied by 4-5 elderly persons of the family and of the village. The bride along with a few elderly ladies viz., aunt and her friends would visit the place of the groom. The marriage would be solemnized at the groom's place. The bride's side need not spend anything except giving few new clothes to the groom. Droupadi and Shyam tied the knot in the Pahadpur village of Kusumi block, in the ancestral home of Shyam Charan Murmu on 11 June 1980. Shyam Charan Murmu was the fourth child of Laxman Murmu and Dhani Murmu. He had three elder sisters, namely, Champa Murmu, Delha Murmu, Sugi Murmu and a younger sister Ganga Murmu. He was the only son of his parents. He possessed a good deal of landed property in Pahadpur which is one kilometre away from Badampahar, the headquarter of the Kusumi block.

Badampahar is situated in a mining belt abundant in iron ore. The area is the rich repository of very high-grade hematite ores. The iron ores would be ported from Badampahar Iron Mine to Tata Steel's second venture next to nearby Gorumahisani Iron Mine. Legendary Jamsetji Nusserwanji Tata had established both, which commenced operations in 1908 and 1922 respectively. Badampahar was connected through rails to facilitate the transport of iron ore. The availability of iron ore has made the place famous in the nation. The rail facility was also developed to port iron ore to Jamshedpur.

Shyam was a polite and friendly person. After marriage, he gladly accepted Droupadi's request to take care of her parents and brothers. This resulted in a strong bonding as they spent more time in each other's company. Droupadi Tudu changed her surname to Murmu after her marriage and came to be known as Droupadi Murmu. She then bid adieu to Delha and other friends in Unit 4 AG colony to stay in a quarter in Sastri Nagar, Bhubaneswar with her husband. Shyam Charan's elder sister who was not married then would stay there with them to take care of the household.

Droupadi's mother-in-law was a little sceptical as to how Droupadi could manage the office work, household and rearing of children in future especially when her husband would get a transfer every third year as a banker. However, Droupadi continued to manage exceptionally well. Shyam Charan was a very understanding husband. He respected his wife and her priorities. When she would help her parents and brothers, Shyam Charan would encourage the same and never try to interfere in her decisions. This made both of them an ideal couple.

In due course of time, Dangi also got married to Sankha Charan Tudu who was working in the Odisha State Secretariat. "I was calling Shyam babu as brother as he and I are Murmu. Similarly, Droupadi calls my husband Sankha Charan Tudu her brother as both of them are Tudus. We had a wonderful family relationship, and we would stand for each other in good and bad times", her best friend Dangi would say. Sankha Charan Tudu retired as the Deputy Secretary, Department of Information and Public Relations and Dangi retired as the Chief Accounts officer. Droupadi worked for a period of four years from 1979 to 1983 in the Secretariat of Government of Odisha.

Delha married Raj Kishore Soren, an officer in State Bank of India in 1981 hailing from Jashipur, Mayurbhanj. Droupadi gifted clothes to both of them which were bought from a cloth shop situated in Master Canteen, Bhubaneswar. Delha had also attended her marriage and gifted clothes. Those days, the simple gifts and one's presence would be considered extremely precious. Both Raj Kishore and Shyam Charan were bank officers and extremely friendly. They developed a strong bond between them.

It is said that, with the birth of the child a mother is born. Motherhood is a divine blessing to humanity. Droupadi and Shyam were blessed with a daughter on February 4, 1981. Born in their familial home at Pahadpur village, it was a normal delivery and both mother and daughter were keeping good health. As per the tradition, she was named after her paternal grand-mother Dhani. Fondly called Mama, she brought immense joy to her parents and family. After availing a few months of maternity leave, Droupadi, with her daughter Mama returned to Bhubaneswar to re-join the office at Odisha state secretariat. Droupadi would keep the child under her sister-in-law's care. She would cook and go to her office leaving her child at home. Shyam Charan was posted in Karanjia branch of the Bank of India, Mayurbhanj.

In the same year in 1981, Droupadi lost her father, Biranchi Narayan. He had been suffering from tuberculosis. Both the sons of Biranchi were too young to take care of the family. Diku was still in school. The newly married Droupadi had to take care of her family by giving solace to mother Singo and to her two brothers.

Though Droupadi became a mother at a young age, she managed home and office with elan. Moreover, after the sudden demise of her father, she took care of her parents' family as and when required. She learnt to take personal and professional responsibilities at a young age. Her husband also supported her. Even though she was a very competent and accomplished lady, being away from her family would always sadden her. Bhubaneswar was also quite far off from Mayurbhanj and would take eight hours to reach by bus. In September 1983, Droupadi joined her husband in Karanjia. She was also pregnant with her second child then. Since Karanjia was near her parental home as well as the home of her in-laws, the family members would join them to help, and it was comfortable for her to manage unlike in Bhubaneswar. Those days, Shyam was posted mostly in Mayurbhanj and later in Bihar (now Jharkhand). She was in the process of making up her mind to quit the job to take care of the children along with her husband Shyam.

The genealogy of Shyam Charan Murmu till 2022 is given.

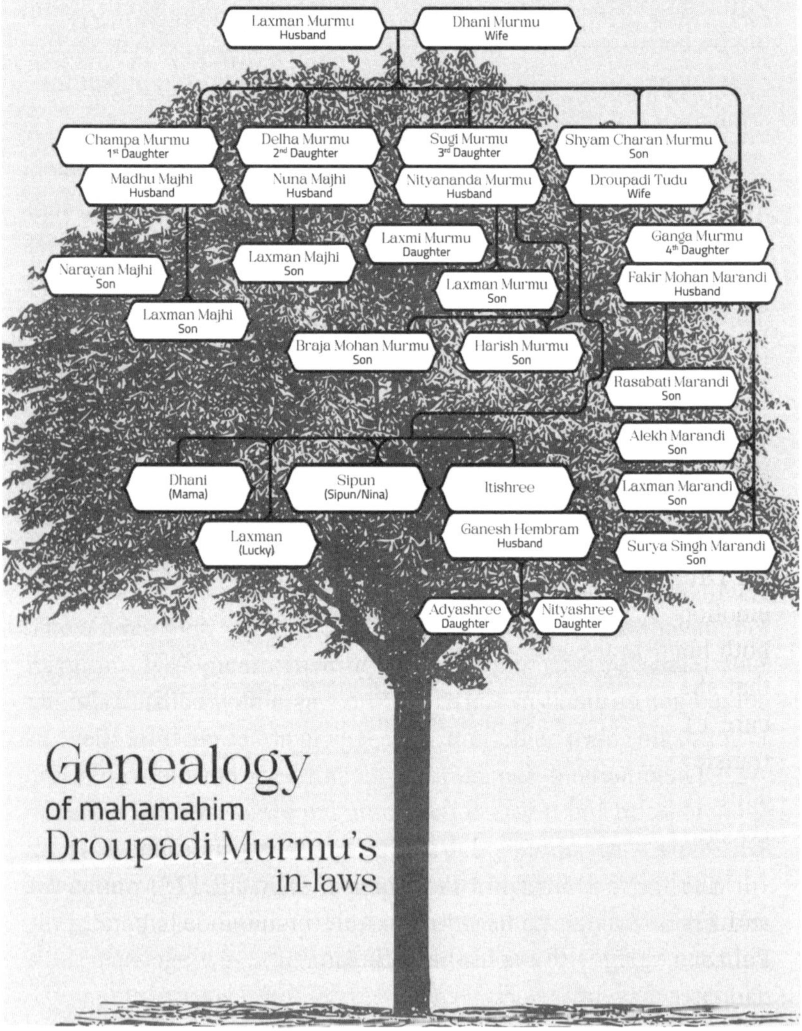

Genealogy of mahamahim Droupadi Murmu's in-laws

Chapter - 5

Home, Harmony & Happiness (1983-1994)

Shyama Charan was posted to various branches of the Bank of India in Mayurbhanj viz., Karanjia, Sukruli, Raruan, and Rairangpur for a decade from 1983 to 1994.

While in Karanjia, in a drastic turn of unfortunate event, their toddler daughter Mama fell sick. She was hospitalized and treatment was started immediately. However, the three-year-old toddler succumbed to the illness leaving the young couple and the entire family in shock. This was a moment of unprecedented despair for Droupadi. She broke down completely. It took a toll on her emotional health as she could not muster enough courage to manage both home and office all by herself. Her mother-in-law also felt that she would not be able to handle a government job and take care of the family simultaneously. Shyam Charan would be transferred to different places and their life would be very frenetic. This resulted in Droupadi making the decision to quit her government job in order to take care of her family.

She came to Karanjia in September 1983. Her second child and first son, Laxman (Lucky) was born on 4 February 1984 in Pahadpur. This was exactly three years after the birth of her first daughter. This was such a coincidence. This was also a normal delivery, and the child was a healthy one. She never went back to work after that as memories of her daughter Mama would haunt her and she was very melancholic. She tendered her resignation from Karanjia as it would be extremely arduous for her to manage home and office single-handedly away from her family and hometown. In her hometown, her family would be there to help her out. She started living with her husband in the places of his postings.

Dhani Marandi, daughter of her uncle Dasmat Marandi was born on 10 June 1984. Dasmat was the youngest among four siblings in the household of Droupadi's maternal family. Her mother, Singo, was the eldest sister and followed by two elder sisters and one brother. She was Droupadi's first cousin.

After a gap of one year and eight months, her second son Biranchi Narayan Murmu (Sipun or Nina) was born in Karanjia on 21 October 1985. The delivery of the third child was also a normal one. Both mother and son were healthy. With frequent transfers as a banker, Shyam Charan and Droupadi would live with their two sons in Sukruli and then in Raruan villages of Mayurbhanj district. The children had not started going to school then. They were healthy, growing well and hardly ever fell sick, reminisces Dr. Pradipta Kumar Mohapatra, paediatrician, who was working as a medical officer in Sukruli and was Droupadi's neighbour. His wife Rajashri Mohapatra and Droupadi would often knit woollen sweaters together. They would knit using colourful yarns sitting on a *Daudia Khata* (rope cot) together in the courtyard. Droupadi loved knitting since her childhood.

Life for the young couple had its share of interesting incidents. In the summer vacation of the following year, Shyam Charan was in the Raruan branch of Bank of India. Once when he was commuting on a motorcycle and in Jhalgunguri ghat, his motorcycle broke down. He was walking while pulling the bike. However, since it was a jungle route, the traffic was very thin in the area, and he could find no help. The heat made him feel breathless and thirsty. He began chewing Sal leaves to save himself from dehydration. At this critical juncture, Delha, her husband, her two-year-old daughter and six-month-old who were on the way to their hometown to spend the vacation from their workplace at Bhubaneswar spotted Shyam Charan from a distance and stopped their motorcycle. The sight of them brought a lease of life to Shyama Charan. They offered him water which he was in immediate need of. Delha's husband brought a clutch and the pad for his motorcycle from the Kashipur market. Shyama Charan could fix his motorcycle and finally drove home with immense gratitude.

The news of the demise of the former Minister and Droupadi's uncle Karthik Chandra Majhi came on 3 March 1987. Droupadi was sad. She was in Raruan village of Mayurbhanj and at an advanced stage of her pregnancy. Her fourth child and youngest daughter Itishree was born on 22 April 1987 in Pahadpur. She was also named after her maternal grandmother Singo. All Droupadi's children were extremely healthy in their childhood and were delivered normally. All the births except that of Sipun had taken place in her in-law's home in Pahadpur.

Soon after, the family shifted to Rairangpur on the transfer of her husband to the Rairangpur branch of Bank of India located near the Rairangpur Sub-Divisional Hospital in a rented building of S.N. Patnaik adjacent to the author's home. Drouapdi would lead the life of a homemaker in Rairangpur as well. The young

Ward No. 2, Rairangpur residence of Droupadi Murmu and her husband Shyam Charan Murmu

couple decided to settle in Rairangpur and purchased property in ward no.2, Baidaposi of Rairangpur and started living there. Some portion of their property was leased out to a Gramya bank. Their permanent residence was located adjacent to the highway of Rairangpur to Jamshedpur.

Droupadi with her youngest daughter Itishree

All her three children had started going to school. Both the boys were studying in the Mahuldiha U.G.M.E. School. Later they studied in Rairangpur High School. Droupadi would monitor their studies at home and make sure they took their education seriously. She valued education above everything and was a good teacher. Often, she would spend time with her children teaching them herself, helping them with their homework and projects. She would make use of singing and acting to make learning much more interesting for her kids.

Shyam Charan was transferred again to Jharkhand. Continuous change of place affected the children's education. So, while Droupadi would stay with the children in Rairangpur, Shyam Charan would visit them on weekends and holidays. Dhani Marandi, Droupadi's maternal cousin and the daughter of her uncle Dasmat Marandi who was also studying in class six, joined them in Rairangpur. She was studying in the same class as that of Sipun. Fondly called as Dhani Mausi (aunt), she would also go to Kanyshram School (now Government SSD Girls High School) at Rairangpur, near their residence. Later she would live with them.

In Karanjia, there used to be a sweeper whose name was Biranchi. He would drink to the brim and would sleep below a bench. Everyone would laugh at Biranchi. So, Droupadi's younger son did not like the fact that he was also called Biranchi. He had been named Biranchi after his maternal grandfather according to the Santhal tradition. The family decided to call him in by his pet name Sipun after that. Some relatives would call him Nina fondly.

As the children were growing and Droupadi was receiving help from her family, she decided to pursue her dream of teaching and serving people. She knew that teaching and being in politics would enable her to fulfil her childhood dream. In 1994, her younger brother Diku appeared for the matriculation examination. She would guide him in his studies. Diku started staying with Droupadi often. Though she was not around in their village Uparbeda during his childhood, the two siblings bonded well when he grew up. Shyam Charan was also fond of his brother-in-law, Diku. Droupadi, her three children, her cousin Dhani, and brother Diku would stay in her Baidaposi, Rairangpur residence. Shyam Charan would come on holiday once or twice a month when he was posted outside Rairangpur. There was happiness, and camaraderie in the ambience. This was one of the happiest times in Droupadi's life, as she raised her children and as a homemaker. As a mother, she was very conscious of her responsibilities.

She also took care of her brothers, her mother, and the extended family. Her younger brother Bhagat (Pata) had also married Chudamani by then. The couple were blessed with two sons Biranchi and Dularam. It was confusing to see another Biranchi in the family with his son and nephew bearing the same name, but it is customary for Santhals to name the grandchild with the name of their grandparent.

Droupadi's mother Singo, Pata, Chudamani and two sons were residing in Droupadi's ancestral home where Droupadi was born. They had renovated the house and added a few rooms to it. They would visit Rairangpur to see Droupadi as Singo was very fond of Droupadi's children. Droupadi would also visit her home with her husband and children during festivals, spending the whole day in the village. She was very fond of her mother and always looked for opportunities to spend time with her. They would perform rituals, and feast together. Her children were accustomed to the rural lifestyle and seamlessly adjusted to it. In fact, they loved to spend time in the village. She had taught her children the values of simple living. The children were not pampered and not extravagant in their needs. Though Shyam Charan was a bank officer, the family believed in modest living. They helped their extended family as and when necessary.

Since Shyam Charan was the only son in a family of five siblings, he had to take care of his parents, get his sisters married, and take care of the family cultivation and property along with his banking job with frequent transfers. He also had a big, landed property in Pahadpur. A few of his sisters were also in their home in Pahadpur even after their marriage. His eldest sister, Champa Murmu was married to Madhu Majhi and had two sons, Narayan and Laxman. His second sister, Delha was married to Nuna Majhi and had one son Laxman Majhi. His third sister, Sugi Murmu was married to Nityananda Murmu having one daughter and three sons namely, Laxmi, Laxman, Braja Mohan, and Harish respectively. These three sisters were elder to him. His younger and fourth sister, Ganga Murmu was married to Fakir Mohan Marandi and had four children viz. Rasabati, Alekh, Laxman, Surya Singh. Thus, there were eleven nephews and nieces who would visit Shyam and Droupadi.

Beside this the Santhals have a great love for festivals and community living. Often, they gather together to celebrate in Makar Parab, Uda Parab, Bandna (Deepavali), Sports competitions, Chhau dance, theatres, *kamaan ghar* (rituals for the departed soul), marriage, weekly *haats* etc. Though there are societal biases towards a male child in comparison to females, the society practices a kind of equality by giving rights to women.

During this period, Droupadi did not have to face any discrimination and turbulence and led a contented life.

Chapter - 6

A Teacher's Transformation through Integral Education (1994-97)

The Integral Education (IE) propounded by the Divine Mother and Sri Aurobindo Ghosh under the aegis of Sri Aurobindo society is meant to revolutionize the prevailing education system and to create holistic conscientious human beings by awakening the fullest potentials of students. With a motto to create the future, the focus is given for a strong, supple, healthy body; a sensitive but emotionally refined energetic persona; a far sighted and intelligent human being; subtler spiritual qualities that unify and harmonize the being around the child's inmost truth or soul (Sri Aurobindo Society, 2022). It is such a historic coincidence that the first Sri Aurobindo Study circle in Odisha was started in Rairangpur in 1949. The second was established in the residence of Sri Lalit Mohan Ghose, Bhasakos lane, Cuttack in 1950. There were approximately 1,00,000 students, 5,000 brothers and sisters in Sri Aurobindo Integral Education Centres in Odisha (The Mother's work in Orissa, 2007-2011).

Approximately 27 acres of land in ward no.13 was purchased by the Sri Aurobindo Society with the initiative of Sushil Chandra Das, a great devotee who was a lawyer by profession. A portion of the land purchased was handed over to the Government of Odisha to establish a government run Aurobindo Upper Primary School in 1955. Since 1949, weekly meditation had been introduced in the town. The weekly meditation and meetings would be conducted either in the home of Sushil Chandra Das in ward no.15 or in the Aurobindo Upper Primary Government School in ward no.13 till 1984. In 1984, seven classes from kindergarten to standard five had started functioning in the 'Aurobindo Integral Education and Research Centre' with a separate school building. At that time Narendra Panda and Sushil Chandra Das were the president and secretary of the school respectively. Narendra Panda's son Niraj Panda would purchase the office equipment/ furniture needed to start the school. In 2005, classrooms for standard six and seven were added to the school. Presently, the Government runs the Aurobindo Upper Primary functions near the Rairangpur Block office and the land and buildings have been handed over to the Aurobindo Integral Education and Research Centre.

Droupadi Murmu joined as a teacher in the Sri Aurobindo Integral Education & Research Centre, Rairangpur, ward no.13 Rairangpur in 1994. Every morning, she used to walk down to the school from her Baidaposi (ward no.2) home, two kilometres away with her youngest daughter Itishree who was studying in the school. Itishree was seven when she joined the school and had her primary education there. Droupadi's colleague Kalpana Mohanty (Tuni) would accompany her from Guru Gomke Pandit Raghunath Murmu square. There is a very old Shri Punyeswar Mahadev temple in the square which they would often visit. They would go to the school enroute the Sri Sathya Sai temple located in ward no. 3 and offer obeisance to the divine lotus feet of Swami. Those days, classes till standard five were held in the school. Her two sons Laxman and Biranchi were studying in higher classes and were going to Mahuldiha UGME School near their home. Her husband, Shyama Charan Murmu was transferred from Bank of India Rairangpur branch to Bhandra Branch in Lohardaga district of Jharkhand. Bhandra is approximately 60 kilometres from Jharkhand state capital Ranchi and 260 kilometres from hometown Rairangpur. He would visit Rairangpur once or twice a month as he had few holidays. Droupadi would take care of the three children. She would get up early at 4 AM, would cook, finish household work, and get the three children ready for school. Then she would start with the youngest daughter for her workplace. Droupadi, Kalpana, and Itishree would reach school by 6.45 AM. The school hours would be from 7 AM to 12 noon. Kalpana was a music teacher in the school. One day, Droupadi was late to school and the school gate was closed. She chose to go back and was never late to the school ever. She would be always punctual, a quality worth imbibing.

Sri Aurobindo Integral Education & Research Center, Rairangpur

The time spent at the Aurobindo Integral School, Rairangpur is most eventful for Droupadi Murmu as she was exposed to the great philosophical ideologies on education propounded by Sri Aurobindo and the Mother. The experiences of selfless human and educational learnings have been ingrained in a manner that she became the embodiment of these values. Even after a century of the teachings, these values shaped the persona of a human who has since adorned the highest office of our great nation. Such is the contribution of Sri Aurobindo and Mother to the world.

Sri Aurobindo Ghosh (August 15, 1872 – December 5, 1950) who is popularly known as 'Sri Aurobindo' is among the greatest educationists of all time apart from being a poet, patriot, sage, and a philosopher. Sri Aurobindo and the Mother were the founders of Integral Education which promises to ensure holistic growth of a student at the level of body, mind and soul. According to this method, there are five elements of education viz., physical, vital, mental, psychic, and spiritual.

The first element, physical education, aims to train the child ever since its birth on disciplines pertaining to food, sleep, and evacuation. It is observed that great human potentials are hindered by small troubles in learning these basics of life. Learning it early is the key to a successful life. It deals with three principal aspects: self-control and discipline of the functioning of the body; an integral, methodical, and harmonious development of all the parts and movements of the body; and correction of deformities and defects if any.

The second aspect, vital education teaches the proper development and use of sense organs as the child grows. This element concerns the awareness and control of the character, resulting in its transformation.

The third element, mental education enables a student to reach high in life. Ideally, it is considered that there are five phases to it. However, it may happen that some phases happen simultaneously. The first is the development of the power of concentration and the development of attention. The second phase is the development of the capacities of expansion, widening, complexity and richness.

The third is the organization of one's ideas around a central idea, a higher ideal or a supremely luminous idea that will serve as a guiding light. The fourth being thought-control, rejection of undesirable thoughts and to be able to think whatever one wants and whenever one wants. The fifth aspect is the blossoming of a mental silence, calm and serene state of mind with total receptivity to inspirations radiating from the higher state of being.

The fourth and fifth elements are psychic and spiritual education, where we come across the challenge of the true motive of existence, the purpose of our life on earth, the discovery to which this life must lead and the result of that discovery: the consecration of the individual to his eternal principle.

Sri Aurobindo said, the purpose of education is to develop latent potentialities, harmonious living of individuals with the society, and integrating oneself with the higher self. A teacher must develop in four levels viz., Chitta or mental consciousness, Manas or Mind, Intelligence and Knowledge to develop the conscience. *Taittiriya Upanishad* described that *Pancha Kosha* (five sheaths) form the human consciousness. These are *Annamaya kosha* (physical body consisting of food); *Pranamaya kosha* (The breath or vital force); *Manomaya kosha* (mind or mental energy); *Vijnanamaya kosha* (knowledge or supramental level according to Sri Aurobindo) and *Anandamaya* (Sat-Chit-Ananda meaning Truth, Consciousness, and Bliss). The mind exists as a separate sheath altogether and is called the mental sheath, which incorporates the memory, reflective and sensory functions of the mind. All five of these coexist within the human and interweave to create the potentiality for evolution that we experience as our spiritual aspiration. (Sri Aurobindo,1940). *Antahkarana* (the conscious mentality) is divided into four powers viz., *Chitta* (mental consciousness), *Buddhi* (intelligence), *Manas* (sense mind), *Ahankar* (ego).

Sri Maa had personally laid the foundation of Auroville, an international township endorsed by UNESCO located in Tamil Nadu near the Pondicherry border. It would be a place "where men and women of all countries were able to live in peace and progressive harmony above all creeds, politics and nationalities." Represented by 121 countries, this was inaugurated in 1968 with participation from all the states of India. Integral education is practised in all the Auroville Schools including Mother International and Mirambika situated at New Delhi.

Sri Aurobindo reiterated on the central object of our education, "Most often, we are inculcated with a general shapeless idea &

enthusiasm corresponding to sentiment & haphazard application. The conception is at the root of our Culture: In any country the best education that can be given is to teach them the true nature of the country, its qualities, mission their nation has to fulfil and its true place in the terrestrial concert without the spirit of imitation and without ever losing sight of the genius of one's country."

Every day, the Aurobindo Integral school starts with a morning prayer followed by meditation in the Samadhi Hall of Mother. The teachers would reach 15 minutes early at 6.45 AM to chant *Durga Stotra* (hymns of Goddess Durga) every day. The students would chant the same every Saturday. Draupadi was greatly inspired by the *Durga Stotra* which she would chant as a practice daily. This would bring a great deal of valour in her to face the challenging world and accord solace for the loss of her first toddler daughter.

Samadhi Mandir at Sri Aurobindo Integral Education & Research Center where Droupadi Murmu was working as a voluntary teacher from 1994-1997

English Translation of Durga Stotra prayed every morning by the teachers and students of Aurobindo Integral is as follows:

Matah Durga! Rider on the lion, giver of all strength, Mother, beloved of Shiva! We, born from thy parts of Power, we the youth of India, are seated here in thy temple. Listen, O Mother, descend upon earth, make thyself manifest in this land of India.

Mother Durga! From age to age, in life after life, we come down into the human body, do thy work and return to the Home of Delight. Now too we are born, dedicated to thy work. Listen, O Mother, descend upon earth, come to our help.

Mother Durga! Rider on the lion, trident in hand, thy body of beauty armour-clad, Mother, giver of victory. India awaits thee, eager to see the gracious form of thine. Listen, O Mother, descend upon earth, make thyself manifest in this land of India.

Mother Durga! Giver of force and love and knowledge, terrible art thou in thy own self of might, Mother beautiful and fierce. In the battle of life, in India's battle, we are warriors commissioned by thee; Mother, give to our heart and mind a titan's strength, a titan's energy, to our soul and intelligence a god's character and knowledge.

Mother Durga! India, world's noblest race, lay whelmed in darkness. Mother, thou risest on the eastern horizon, the dawn comes with the glow of thy divine limbs scattering the darkness. Spread thy light, Mother, destroy the darkness.

Mother Durga! We are thy children, through thy grace, by thy influence may we become fit for the great work, for the great Ideal. Mother, destroy our smallness, our selfishness, our fear.

Mother Durga! Thou art Kali, naked, garlanded with human heads, sword in hand, thou slay the Asura. Goddess, do thou slay with thy pitiless cry the enemies who dwell within us, may none remain alive there, not one. May we become pure and spotless; this is our prayer. O Mother, make thyself manifest.

Mother Durga! India lies now in selfishness and fearfulness and littleness. Make us great, make our efforts great, our hearts vast, make us true to our resolve. May we no longer desire the small void of energy, given to laziness, stricken with fear.

Mother Durga! Extend the power of Yoga. We are thy Aryan children, develop in us again the lost teaching, character, strength of intelligence, faith and devotion, force of austerity, power of chastity and true knowledge, bestow all that upon the world. To help mankind, appear, O Mother of the world, dispel all ills.

Mother Durga! Slay the enemy within, then root out all obstacles outside. May the noble heroic mighty Indian race, supreme in love and unity, truth and strength, arts and letters, force and knowledge ever dwell in its holy woodlands, its fertile fields under its sky-scraping hills, along the banks of its pure-streaming rivers. This is our prayer at the feet of the mother. Make thyself manifest.

Mother Durga! Enter our bodies in thy Yogic strength. We shall become thy instruments, thy sword slaying all evil, thy lamp dispelling all ignorance. Fulfil this yearning of thy young children, O Mother. Be the master and drive the instrument, wield the sword and slay the evil, hold up the lamp and spread the light of knowledge. Make thyself manifest.

Mother Durga! When we possess thee, we shall no longer cast thee away; we shall bind thee to us with the tie of love and devotion. Come, Mother, manifest in our mind and life and body.

Come, Revealer of the hero-path. We shall no longer cast thee away. May our entire life become a ceaseless worship of the mother, all our acts a continuous service to the mother, full of love, full of energy. This is our prayer, O Mother, descend upon earth, make thyself manifest in this land of India. ('Hymn to Durga' - English translation of *'Durga Stotra').*

Students and teachers would pray and meditate together, and these were the core values of integral education. Droupadi was also exposed to the timeless wisdom written in the form of books by Sri Aurobindo viz., The Life Divine, Savitri: A Legend and a Symbol, The future evolution of a man, Essays on the Gita, The Synthesis of Yoga, The Human Cycle, Ideal of Human Unity, etc. As a bibliophile, she had keen interest to spend her time reading these books, telling inspiring stories to children. She never spent time on non-productive pursuits. During the closing of the school at 12 Noon, all students would stand class wise in rows to sing "*Vande Mataram*', the national song to instil the nationalistic sentiments in them. Every day the teachers would write the 'Thought of the day' on the black board of each class. The quotes and teachings of Sri Aurobindo and Sri Maa would be written there. These practices inculcated discipline in the students. Such was the popularity of the school that students used to come from Rairangpur Bazaar to study here even though there were other schools nearby.

Droupadi was destined to get a robust grounding on educational philosophy in the school along with seven other teachers namely Sushil Chandra Das (the principal), Indira Otta, Dibakar Mohanta, Rohina Behera, Ranjan Kumar Patra, Kalpana Mohanty, and Prabodh Panda. Bhagirathi Patra and Dillip Giri were the office assistants during the time. Drupad Chandra Dagara, Industrialist and Purna Chandra Mohanta, Lawyer were president and secretary of the managing committee of the school during the time she worked in the school. She rendered voluntary service for a tenure of three years in the school.

Droupadi would teach a range of subjects viz., social science, mathematics, and Odia literature to students from kindergarten to standard five. "She was an adorable teacher, recounts her old student, Lalit Agrawalla, Principal system architect in New Jersey, USA. She taught social science to us in standard four and five and never punished us. She would treat us as her own children and was always soft-spoken." His father Ashok Agrawalla, who owns one of the oldest book shops in Rairangpur also recalls fond memories of parent-teacher meetings. "I have never seen her getting angry, reminisces another student Abhisek Bharatiya who became a geologist, and who was taught Odia literature in standard three by her. She took personal attention and used to remember every student even by their nicknames, decades after as well." Siddhant Bharatiya, geologist, recollects that, "Droupadi Didi was my class teacher in kindergarten II and that was her last year in the school in the 1996-97 academic session. Later, when she became Vice-Chairperson of Raiarangpur Notified Area Council (now Municipality), I received many prizes in quiz and essay competitions held to mark the occasion of *Swayatta Shasan Divas* (Urban Local Self Governance Day) held on 31 August 1999". She had immense clarity and patience while teaching, which was passed on to students and they could grasp the subjects easily. The students were very fond of her because of her motherly affection towards them.

Indira Otta (Buli) worked in the school for 32 years and her father Jagabandhu Otta was also secretary of the study circle (Patha Chakra) for some time. After her bachelor's in arts from Rairangpur College, she joined the school as a teacher to contribute her bit for nation building by creating robust future generations. She reminisces Droupadi's unique skill to dress students in theatre competitions. She would do the makeup and the dressing of the children as many mythological and modern characters with ease. Her uncle Banaju was a great make-up artist in the village. It was from him that Droupadi picked up these skills. She was a great orator with a sharp presence of mind. She would give good speeches on the Independence Day and Republic Day events observed in the school. Shri Aurobindo's Birthday falls on 15 August on the country's Independence Day. Since all the students and teachers would go to the Football Field (now stadium) of Rairangpur to participate in a ceremonial parade conducted by the Sub-division, the school would celebrate the birthday of Sri Maa on 21 February with splendour.

Sri Maa, the Divine mother whose name was Mirra Alfassa was born in Paris on 21 February 1878. In 1914 the mother travelled to Pondicherry (now Puducherry) accompanied by her spouse Paul

Richard, to meet Sri Aurobindo. She reached Pondicherry on 29 March 1914 after a journey of three weeks and on the same day, she met Sri Aurobindo. Sri Maa was his *Shakti* and twin soul. The Mother wrote, "As soon as I saw Sri Aurobindo, I recognized in him the well-known being whom I used to call Krishna. And this is enough to explain why I am fully convinced that my place and my work are near him, in India." On 30 March 1914, Mother wrote in her diary, "It matters little that there are thousands of beings plunged in the densest ignorance, He whom we saw yesterday is on earth; his presence is enough to prove that a day will come when darkness shall be transformed into light, and Thy reign shall be indeed established upon earth".

Gradually, she took charge of Sri Aurobindo Ashram for about half a century and merged into the Divine on 17 November 1973. The school in Rairangpur would observe Mother's arrival in India as '*Aagman Divas*' as well as her date of demise. On 24 November 1926, Sri Maa and Sri Aurobindo had declared the *Siddhi* Day (The Day of Victory). On that day there was the descent of the Sri Krishna Consciousness into the physical world. Every year the Aurobindo Ashram and the schools celebrate the day. The book, 'Who is Mother?' written by Pasupati Bhattacharya and translated into Odia by Bhairab Chandra Mohanty was read by the teachers and students. A chapter of the Nabajyoti magazine was also read by the teachers every day.

This Swadhyay (self-study) made the teachers realise the essence of integral education. Training, discussions of knowledge (*Patha Chakras*) and continuous *Swadhyay* with contemplation is the key to imbibe these timeless virtues gradually and to pass on to the next generations for a better world order as envisioned by Sri Maa and Sri Aurobindo. Self- practice makes the preaching more authentic.

Indira said, "Droupadi had come to my place two-three times while working in the school. Her husband Shyam Charan had also come once to take Homeopathic medicine for some minor ailment from my brother Dr. Dhurjati Otta. He was also a person with humility and always carried an unfading smile. I had also gone to her Baidaposi home a number of times. She was very friendly and when we reminisce, all the fond memories resurface".

Droupadi had a photographic memory. Kalpana Mohanty's nephew Kanha was born as an underweight premature baby during the time they were colleagues in the school. Droupadi would ask about him regularly and would go to see him. She was a gifted teacher. She had excellent communication skills and enormous patience to handle all kinds of students. Droupadi also had a mellifluous voice and would often sing with the students. Her singing was appreciated in the school by one and all. She would prepare students for inter-school debates, singing, drawing, and quiz competitions held during Independence Day, Republic Day, and Swayatta Shasan Dibas etc.

During her tenure in school, the teachers and students would go for a picnic twice a year to nearby Suleipat Dam and Ramatirtha Crocodile Project and temple. Suleipat and Khadakhai dam reservoir are 20 kilometres away and half an hour's journey from the school in Rairangpur. Ramatirtha River is a very picturesque place near Jashipur in the Mayurbhanj district where the Government of Odisha has a Crocodile project. This is approximately 40 kilometres away and a one-hour journey. Tusu Mela and Tusu Parab are also observed there. It is believed that, in *Treta Yuga* Lord Rama Chandra, Devi Sita and brother Laxman had passed through Simlipal forest during their 14 years *Van Vaas* (dwelling in forest). During their journey mother Sita felt tired and sat on a stone near the Ramatirtha river. She washed her face and feet. Since then, the place has become a place of pilgrimage. Nowadays many visit the place for a picnic and for sight-seeing. Droupadi would cut vegetables and would take part in cooking during the picnic as well. She had contributed to almost all verticals in the school, and this made her a very popular teacher even if she spent only three years there.

"The more we advance on the path, the more modest we become and more we see that we have done nothing in comparison to what remains to be done". – The Mother

It was as if the above message was evident in her. Her demeanour was very pleasing and peace loving which prompted her to contribute more and more. The school was managed through the monthly tuition fees paid by the students. Many teachers were getting a very nominal honorarium. Droupadi was not taking any and her services were completely voluntary in nature. Some philanthropists like Ghanashyam Mishra had constructed a few buildings. Droupadi also contributed to the construction & infrastructure development of the school later after leaving the school to join politics. Nevertheless, the modest resources did not deter the will power of the team members of the school. They functioned very efficiently due to the dedication of many teachers like her.

Photo: from Left to Right:Late Rohina Behera, Prabodha Panda, Kalpana Mohanty, Droupadi Murmu, Indira Otta, Ranjan Kumar Patra, Dillip Giri, Late Dibakar Mohanta. Late Sushil Chandra Das (sitting in Chair)

Lipika Das, daughter of late Sushil Chandra Das who was the founding member of Aurobindo Integral School lives in the Sri Aurobindo Ashram in Puducherry. Sushil Chandra Das was the Secretary of the school and acted as the principal also for quite some time. When Mrs Murmu went to visit Puducherry during her presidential campaign in July 2022, she never forgot to meet Ms Das, who has dedicated her life for the divine cause. She has a photographic memory and never forgets her colleagues. Dillip Behera, who continues to serve as the office assistant, recalled once when Droupadi was teaching in kindergarten, a lizard fell on her head. It is a belief that, if the lizard falls on the head, the person attains meteoric rise. He felt it to be true in her case. Everyone in the school had a story to narrate as they liked her pleasant demeanour, humility, and soft-spoken behaviour.

It is said that service to mankind is service to God.' Though she did the job out of her own interest to teach children and learn something in return, this selfless Sadhana (disciplined and dedicated practice) has become a repository of good luck, and opportunities for her. Exposure to the great Sri Aurobindo philosophy was a distant dream for a tribal woman who was leading life as a homemaker in the 1990s. Droupadi has searched for opportunities to gain knowledge in every walk of life which made her great. There could be thirsty people near a well as well. However, she was quite conscious and aware of her surroundings and learnt from the school library and the training imparted to the teachers to practise integral education. It is not surprising that teachers were termed as guides and facilitators by Sri Aurobindo.

On Sundays and other holidays Droupadi would team up with few like-minded women to nurture and popularize the culture and traditions of *Adivasis*. Her contribution to Adibasi Socio Educational and Cultural Association (hereafter, ASECA) is noteworthy. ASECA was established by Guru Gomke Pandit Raghunath Murmu, the inventor of the Ol-Chiki script of Santali language in 1936 under the title 'Ol Samiti'. In 1952, the name was changed to 'Adivasi Lakchar Semled". Few years later it was registered as Adivasi Socio Educational and Cultural Association (ASECA) in the 1960s in Odisha, Bihar and West Bengal and in the 1980s in the state of Assam. It is a socio-cultural, educational, voluntary, and apolitical organization of Santhals in India. She would go for various meetings of ASECA along with her aunt Sabitri Dei.

The trauma of losing her child would haunt her years later. She could never forget the incident even after the birth of her two sons and her youngest daughter. She would always discuss about her with Laxman Soren, her uncle. Laxman Soren was a lawyer and an active member of Rairangpur Bar Association. His wife Sabitri Dei was a school teacher in the Government run Mahuldiha UGME school where Droupadi's sons were studying. Sabitri's daughter Saraswati Soren has fond memories on Droupadi's dedication for ASECA. She served selflessly for the betterment of the socio-cultural life of tribals especially the Santhals. Though ASECA is meant for all the tribals, the involvement of Santhals would be more, it being the majority tribe. Moreover, there are variations in cultures and traditions of other tribes of Mayurbhanj districts as well.

All the teachers in the school would have refreshments together at 9.30 AM in *tiffin chhuti* (break for having small refreshments) like one family. Many would bring delicious snacks from their home. Everyone would share their food. Her teacher colleague Dibakar Mohanta was very hospitable and would enhance the camaraderie among teachers by inviting for impromptu samosa and Aloo (potato) Chop Party in school sourced by the ever - resourceful Dillip, the office assistant. All the teachers and office assistants would come together for refreshments. He encouraged Droupadi to join politics as she had a natural flair to lead. She had an innate tendency to take up responsibilities and Mayurbhanj being a tribal dominated district offered opportunities for tribal women leaders especially in local governance after the promulgation of 74th Constitutional amendment in 1992.

She was later introduced to Rabindra Nath Mohanta, lawyer turned politician whose home was adjacent to the Aurobindo school. Rabindra Nath Mohanta was also a lawyer of Bank of India, Rairangpur branch where her husband Shyama Charan Murmu was working as an officer. He was the Bharatiya Janata Party President of Mayurbhanj district of Odisha from 1996-2005 for two consecutive terms. Once Rabindra Nath Mohanta told another political protégé Navin Kumar Ram that he had discovered a very nice lady candidate to be fielded from ward no.2 in the forthcoming urban local election of Rairangpur NAC. Since his home and Droupadi's school were separated by a 10 feet road, they would often meet to discuss her formal inclusion in the Bharatiya Janata Party. She continued to teach till the beginning of her political career when she was fielded as a candidate by the Bharatiya Janata Party in urban local body election as a councillor in 1997. However, she continued to visit the school on annual days, picnics and other important occasions. She was in touch with each of her colleagues.

God returns manifold what you offer him. This was true in Droupadi's case. In later years, when she became a member of Legislative Assembly from Rairangpur (ST) Constituency and a Minister of State, she offered more than seven lakh rupees in funds for building classrooms and a meditation hall in the school in 2002. Now the school has 70 students and stands as a hallmark of the glorious history of Bharat.

In July 2022, the school was photographed most in its existence of 40 years as journalists googled and thronged to the place with the help of her acquaintances. She continues to work for value education throughout her life and has always been passionate for the cause of creating holistic individuals who have a refined state of being, and control over their senses to transform themselves to serve the nation.

Chapter - 7

Pilgrimage of Politics: Part of 25 years of political life 1997-2010

Even though many people know that Droupadi Murmu's political career started as a ward councillor in 1997, not many are aware that her attempt for becoming a political leader and to serve the society started from the 1992 urban local election of Rairangpur Notified Area Council (NAC). She contested the local election as an independent candidate from ward no.1 in the year 1992, the first election that happened after the 74th Constitutional amendment which provided one third reservation of seats to women candidates in urban local bodies. She had to face a debacle as nobody knew her abilities. She was also new to the town. Her intrinsic will to serve the society was insurmountable but she had to wait for the right opportunity. So, after the defeat in the maiden local election she focussed on her profession of teaching. She continued to work as a teacher in Aurobindo Integral Education and Research Centre of Rairangpur from the year 1994. This was a voluntary assignment for her and she was discharging her duties to the best of her abilities putting her soul into the progress of students. During her free time, she would contribute to the socio-cultural life of Adivasis in association with Adibasi Socio Educational & Cultural Association (hereafter, ASECA). ASECA, an acclaimed social organisation of Indian tribals.

Sri Aurobindo Integral Education and Research Centre at Rairangpur and the residence of eminent lawyer and BJP district president of Mayurbhanj, Rabindra Nath Mohanta is separated by a narrow lane. Bikash Medical Store, named after his only son, would be the hub of local politics and all the strategies of expansion of the Bharatiya Janata Party would be decided in the courtyard of his residence. The participants of the informal evening sessions were represented by his son Bikash Chandra Mohanta, Navin Kumar Ram (Now State General Secretary of BJP, Odisha), Sanjib Mohanty, Dillip Kumar Singh, Dibakar Mohanta, Shiv Shankar Agarwal, Manoj Das, Sunil Mohanta, Naba Charan Majhi (Now MLA Rairangpur constituency), Pradip Das and Ishan Mishra to name a few. These team members were mostly drawn from business and legal professions that contributed to the growth of the party in the area. The passion and dedication of the team translated into the citizen's mandate in the local, state and the union elections many times during that period. It is said that the tenure of the presidentship of Rabinda Nath Mohanta witnessed the blossoming of the lotus (party symbol of BJP) in the Mayurbhanj district, especially in the Bamanghaty sub- division. The sub-divisional headquarter Rairangpur Assembly constituency has been a bastion of the Indian National Congress (INC) and the Jharkhand Mukti Morcha (JMM) since the Adivasis identified themselves with these parties for more than three assembly elections preceding that of the year 1997.

There were many events, which had a bearing on one another that led to the making of the future President of the nation. Rabindra Nath Mohanta was also the lawyer for the Bank of India where Shyam Charan was the branch manager. Both would connect over *paan* (betel leaves) and puns in the bank. Their bonhomie was infectious. The thought of Droupadi as a party candidate for the local urban election of the year 1997 was mooted in these meetings. Mohanta also knew Droupadi as the niece of Karthik Majhi, former Minister and had met her as a school student in Bhubaneswar a few decades ago. Rairangpur NAC had 15 wards out of which five were reserved for women candidates after the 74th Constitutional amendment, 1992, paving a way for greater participation of women in urban local governance. The ward no.2 was also reserved for a lady candidate. Shyam Charan who had a great affinity for politics, wholeheartedly supported this political opportunity for his wife. Her brother Diku and wife Sakramani were also supportive of her. The three children Laxman (Lucky), Biranchi (Sipun), and Itishree (Iti) also encouraged her to pursue her political career.

Droupadi was offered a ticket to contest from ward no. 2 of Rairangpur NAC in the urban local election in the year 1997. She campaigned diligently for the election. Her colleagues from the Aurobindo school, especially Dibakar Mohanta supported the campaign. Droupadi won the election as the ward councillor. Her family, and party workers celebrated her victory with much fanfare.

However, destiny had bigger things in store for her. The Vice-Chairpersonship of the NAC was also reserved for a woman. She was nominated for the post by the party leadership. She became the Vice-chairperson of Rairangpur NAC in 1997. It is pertinent to mention here that, both the councillor and the vice-chairperson posts were reserved for women but not for scheduled tribes. In the same election, Raj Kishore Das became the Chairman of the Rairangpur NAC for the second consecutive time. Droupadi continued as the Vice-Chairperson for three years. Her work on maintenance of hygiene and sanitation of the township won her accolades from far and wide. She would visit all the 15 wards of Rairangpur on her scooter to supervise sanitation work. She became a well-known political personality in the town within a short span of time owing to her dedication and sincerity. Because of her amicable nature, she bonded well with the chairman and the other team members of the urban local body to foster better public service delivery and governance in the township.

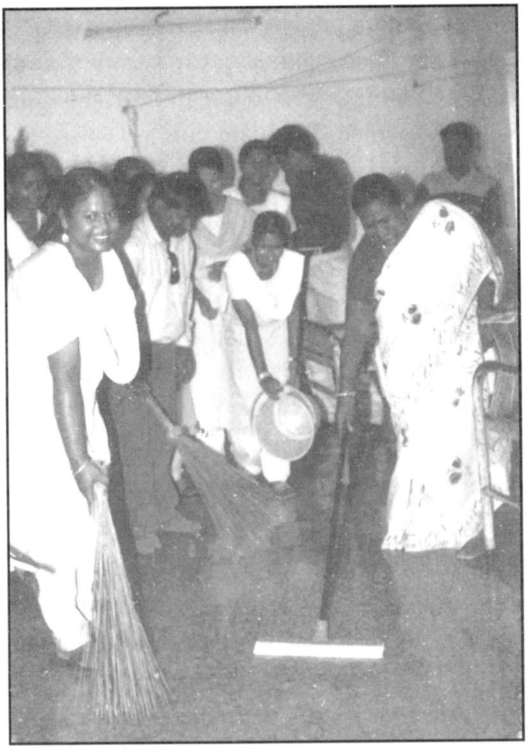

Droupadi Murmu participating in cleaning camps

The 12th Odisha Legislative Assembly election was due in the year 2000. A major political change was awaiting the Odisha Government at that time. One of the longest serving, Chief Minister of three terms, considered invincible by many, Janaki Ballabh Patnaik was asked to resign by the party leadership after an unprecedented unfortunate incident in February 1999. Subsequently, the 11th Odisha Legislative Assembly witnessed two chief ministers namely Giridhar Gamang and Hemananda Biswal for 292 days and 90 days respectively before the upcoming assembly election. The frequent changes of leadership in Odisha by the Congress high command led to a lack of confidence among the voters for the INC. Certain unpleasant incidents, and anti-incumbency led to the beginning of the downfall of the grand old party in the state.

On 15 March 1997, the legendary Bhoomi Putra Bijayananda (Biju) Patnaik who was Chief Minister twice and was in Janata Dal in the later part of his life, passed away. After his demise, his younger son Naveen Patnaik who was a litterateur was invited by Mr Biju Patnaik's old time proteges. Naveen had to concede to the sincere requests of the partymen by agreeing to shift to Bhubaneswar from New Delhi. The fierce campaigning started, as Odisha was starting a new era of Biju Janata Dal - Bharatiya Janata Party (BJD-BJP) coalition under the stewardship of Naveen Patnaik. The voters were in the mood for a change in the state. The assembly election of 2000 broke all perceptions and prejudices by bringing in a new era of coalition politics.

Seeing her dedication and good work, Vice-Chairperson Droupadi was offered a party ticket to contest for the Rairangpur (ST) constituency in 2000, merely three years into her political career. Rabindra Nath Mohanta, lawyer turned BJP leader and Party President of Mayurbhanj district played a pivotal role in choosing her candidature amidst a lot of speculation in political quarters. History was created when the BJD-BJP coalition government won the people's mandate with overwhelming support from the voters of the state. Droupadi Murmu from BJP, Laxman Majhi from INC, and Braja Mohan Hansdah from Jharkhand Mukti Morcha (JMM) had a fierce electoral battle in the Rairangpur (ST) constituency.

In the process of seat sharing in the BJD-BJP pre-poll alliance, the Rairangpur constituency was allocated to the BJP. That meant that no BJD candidate would be fielded for the constituency. Draupadi won with 25,110 votes, a share of 34.15% votes when Laxman and Braja polled 20,542 (27.93%) and 10,485 (14.26%) votes respectively. She became the first lady MLA to win from the Rairangpur assembly constituency. This elevated her to a very special position, and she bagged the post of Minister of state under the Chief Ministership of Naveen Patnaik. The BJD-BJP coalition won the election with a majority by winning 68 seats (29.39% vote share) and 38 seats (18.19% vote share) respectively with a total of 106 seats of a 147-member house. Even though the incumbent INC under the Chief Ministership of Hemanand Biswal had the highest vote share of 33.77%, it could garner only 26 seats. This paved a way for a change of rule in the state.

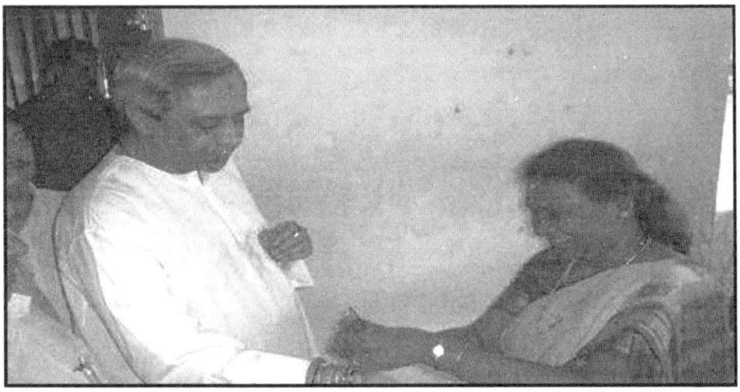

Newly elected MLA Droupadi Murmu tying a Rakhi to Naveen Patnaik, Chief Minister of Odisha in the year 2000

She was chosen by the leadership to the post of Minister of state with Independent Charge for Department of Commerce and Transport from 6 March 2000 to 6 August 2002, and Department of Fisheries and Animal Resources Development from 6 August 2002 to 16 May 2004. In a short span of three years, Droupadi witnessed a meteoric rise from a voluntary school teacher to a ward councillor, to a Member of the Legislative Assembly, and then on to become a Minister of state in Odisha. Very soon, she would become a familiar face to 45 million Odias of the state. It was as if she was born to lead and that she was in the right place at the right time. Her rise seemed like a fairy tale to many, and soon she emerged as a significant political force to reckon with.

On her visit to Bhubaneswar, after being elected as MLA for the first time and having become a Minister, she would stay in the Odisha State guest house for a few months as allotment of government quarters took some time. She once called Delha (Muni Apa) to enquire whether she could make a visit to the latter's place

Inauguration at Kukudimundi village of Rairangpur Constituency on 17.11.2002

to have home cooked lunch. Delha prepared Pakhala, Saga (a dish prepared from green leaves) and all her favourite dishes. Droupadi and a few party workers relished the lunch, and this is one memory which both cherish till date. Delha had also invited her to the Annual Sports Event at her ancestral home Chheligodhuli in Jashipur block of Mayurbhanj. Every year on 6 February, annual sports are held in that village. Droupadi would honour the invitation and attend the event as a guest while she was the minister. She was committed to honour every invite in her constituency. She would grace every small and big programme of her constituency, be it a football match, village sports, cultural programmes, prize khia (feast after prize ceremony), marriage, thread ceremony, 21 days ceremony of a new-born, *kamaan ghar* (rituals for the departed soul), functions in a school, college functions, ASECA programme etc. Eventually she became a part of the lives of all her constituents attending all functions-sometimes to celebrate and sometimes to grieve.

Droupadi's accessibility and simplicity made her very popular in a very short span of time. It is said that she has visited every village of her constituency. Most of these visits meant long tiring walks for hours She was however no stranger to walking. A regular regimen of walking had kept her extremely fit and healthy. She walked extensively in the inaccessible Chadhei Pahadi village under Bijatala block. Bijatala block was under Rairangpur assembly constituency those days. Presently, it is under Saraskana assembly constituency after delimitation. "The lack of development coupled with the inaccessibility of the location led to the rise of extremists trying to take advantage of the situation. They were a possible threat to the locals. Droupadi was instrumental in us pursuing the relevant government scheme for the construction of roads. There were virtually no roads to the area. Often, I commuted on a motorcycle and the spoke of the motorcycle needed to be replaced after each visit", Navin Kumar Ram recollected.

Droupadi Murmu with her political protégé Navin Kumar Ram in Rairangpur Constituency on 14.11.2005

Once, when she was a minister, Droupadi Murmu was invited to a programme in the village Basantpur inside the Similipal forest area. There was a drama competition organised by the villagers. The programme was to last the entire night till the early hours of the following day when the prizes would be distributed. She left her Rairangpur home at 3 AM along with her team members to reach by 5 AM to distribute the prizes. The inhabitants were Vanvasis (forest dwellers). Eating only a little Mudhi (puffed rice) and Gur (jaggery) to satiate their hunger, they waited through the night for their leader to visit them. This was a testimony to the love and adulation they had for an ethical political leader in a tribal district.

During her first meeting as the Minister of Transport and Commerce, she gathered information regarding the functions of the department, and she would pick up information from the officials of the department in charge of collecting taxes etc. in lieu of the services rendered to the community. She brought in reforms which boosted the revenue collection of the department considerably. These actions brought many laurels to her as a new minister. Keen observation and commitment to excel are Droupadi's winning traits. She is an eternal learner and because of her etiquette and manners she became everyone's favourite.

One of the first initiatives of Droupadi Murmu after becoming a minister of state was to construct a bridge on the Kanhu River, something she had envisioned for more than three decades. This would enable the road communication from Hatbadla- Kaduani Chhak to her ancestral village Uparbeda and many other villages like Tentoposi, Dubulabeda, Baliadhipa etc. The foundation to the Kanhu River Bridge was laid on 28 September 2000 in the presence of Droupadi Murmu and Salkhan Murmu, Member of Parliament (LS) from Mayurbhanj Parliamentary constituency. It was like a dream come true when the Kanhu River Bridge became operational. She inaugurated the bridge on 20 March 2005 in the presence of Biswabhushan Harichandan, Minister, Rural Development, Law and Industries of the Government of Odisha during the 2nd term of the BJD-BJP Coalition Government under the Chief Ministership of Naveen Patnaik. It is now known as Kanhu Setu (Kanhu bridge) and 'Kaduani-Uparbeda Rasta'. Needless to say, the villagers were very happy. This paved the way for better socio-economic well-being for those who longed for decades to see the bridge function.

Droupadi Murmu was also instrumental in the construction of one more bridge on the Guria River joining Badmouda and Hatia villages under the Hatia gram panchayat of the Rairangpur block.

Inauguration of Kanhu Setu in the presence of Biswabhushan Harichandan, Minister, Rural Development, Law and Industries of the Government of Odisha on 20.03.2005

This is also one of the significant bridges of the constituency which joined some remote and inaccessible villages. The villagers were facing endless hassles in commuting especially during the rainy season. Some villagers had to take circuitous routes of 7-10 kilometres. These initiatives eased communication by benefitting thousands of her constituents.

During her tenure as the Minister of Transport and Commerce, she gave a proposal for an Additional Regional Road Transport Office (RTO) at Rairangpur. Mayurbhanj being the largest district of the state, many areas like Tiring, Bahalada are more than 100 kilometres away from its district headquarters Baripada and people found it inconvenient to commute just for administrative needs. The establishment of an RTO at Rairangpur made it convenient for people from Rairangpur, Jashipur, Karanjia, Bahalada, Tiring, Hatbadla, Gorumahisani etc. She made her mark as a visionary leader, by adopting novel methods of governance with ease aimed towards the upliftment of the constituency.

Droupadi worked more assiduously after being the minister to honour the faith reposed in her by the state. There was a reshuffling of the portfolio on 6 August 2002, and she was made the minister of state (independent charge), Department of Fisheries and Animal Resources Development. She initiated a great deal of developmental work. She proposed a Livestock Aid Centre under the department of F&ARD, Odisha at Uparbeda. This was constructed by the Integrated Tribal Development Agency, Rairangpur and inaugurated on 13 October 2006 during her second term as MLA. She had established two milk collection centres known as Bulk Milk Cooler (BMC) in Rairangpur and Hatbadla to collect milk from farmers' cooperatives.

The constituents of Rairangpur were very happy as they re-elected her for the second consecutive term in 2004 on a BJP seat. However, this time the electoral battle was keenly contested, and she won with a narrow margin of 42 votes from her nearest

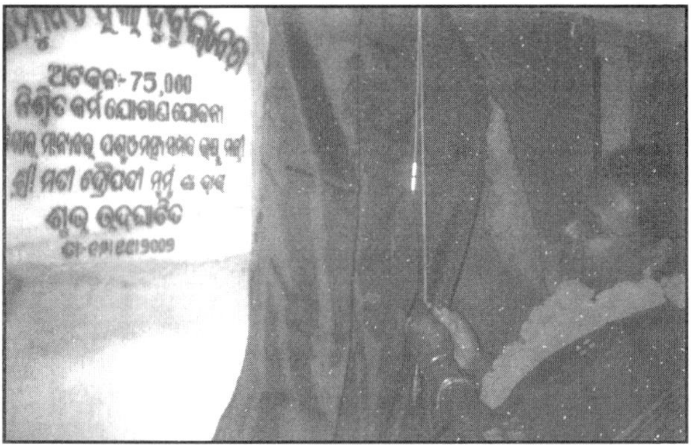

Inauguration of Community Hall in Dubulabeda village of Rairangpur Constituency on 17.11.2002

JMM competitor Rama Chandra Murmu. While she received 29,295 votes Rama Chandra Murmu polled 29,253 votes and the INC candidate and former MLA (1995) Laxman Majhi got 22,551 votes. The victory touched the hearts of people close to her, those who had supported her and helped her retain her seat. She was the leader who was available in their good and bad days and gained popularity because of her availability and sense of belongingness. Retaining the seat was a huge responsibility for the party as well, especially when there was a pre-poll alliance between two parties.

This time also Naveen Patnaik became the Chief Minister for the second consecutive term winning 61 (BJD) and 32 (BJP) seats totalling 94. This time also INC had the highest vote share of 34.82% as the single largest party in comparison to BJD at 27.36% and BJP at 17.11%. Though INC won 38 seats which was 12 seats higher over last assembly, forming a government seemed a distant dream for the centenarian party. The party's presence as the most influential ideology block was gradually waning like the sea recedes in Chandipur. Naveen was emerging as a formidable leader, much like a waxing moon.

There was a strategically important airstrip in Rairangpur (Dandbose), situated in Bamanghaty subdivision and was constructed by the British Government during the period of World War II. Spread over 61 acres of land, and a runway of 750 metres, the airstrip is the second most prominent airstrip of Mayurbhanj after Rajabasa. This airstrip was maintained by the Works department of Government of Odisha. Odisha had twelve airstrips maintained by the Government and six airstrips maintained by private organisations. Dandbose Air strip was managing Dakota type airplanes of which had been used extensively during the second World War by the allies. However, in recent times, it was mostly used as a helipad for helicopters. The encroachment started happening on the land. At that time, Droupadi was the chairperson of the standing committee of the Department of Home, Government of Odisha. By virtue of that position, she facilitated the construction of the boundary wall and of the runaway of the important airstrip, thereby saving it from misuse. Dandbose is also the native place of Guru Gomke Pandit Raghunath Murmu, the founder of Ol Chiki script which had given a distinction to the Santali language.

During her tenure as the chairperson of the standing committee of the Department of Home, Government of Odisha, she visited the jails in Odisha and was moved to see the plight of some of the prisoners. She observed that many inmates were languishing in jail owing to their inability to hire a lawyer and also their ignorance regarding the judiciary processes. Some inmates did not want to leave jail because they received free food, and free stay. To avoid societal stigma of police custody and judicial interventions they preferred to stay in jail. She suggested prompt judicial help for such needy persons who were in jails because of minor crimes.

Once, during her three-year tenure as the Chairperson of the Standing Committee of the Department of Home, she was travelling back to Bhubaneswar from Rairangpur when she witnessed *Rasta Rok* (roadblock) by the Adivasis of Bisoi protest against some incidents of police high handedness. She halted and had a dialogue with the agitators to know the real cause of the revolt. She immediately intervened and redressed their grievance by speaking to the Principal Secretary, Department of Home, Government of Odisha, the Inspector General of Police, and the Superintendent of Police, Mayurbhanj. She resolved the matter amicably and peacefully on the spot itself. Her timely move of pacifying the rebels and settling the issue dissolved the agitation.

There is a scheme under the planning and convergence department of the state government known as the Member of Legislative Assembly - Local Area Development funds like that of Member of Parliament Local Area Development MPLAD fund in Odisha since 1997-98. An amount of INR 75 lakh is distributed to each MLA for the development of the constituency. Droupadi made it a point that this fund is distributed for upliftment of education, culture and upholding the spiritual quotient of her constituency. The MLALAD fund is distributed to construction of boundaries and buildings of temples, Jaher Garh, schools, bar council building, sports facility, clubs, electrification etc. With the help of MLALAD funds, many villages of Kusumi block have been electrified and clean and safe drinking water has been provided. The list of MLALAD distribution is exhaustive. Some of the prominent distributions include the construction of the boundary wall of Shiva temple of Hatbadla, Sanpakhna, Niranjan, Tambadiha (Jaipur Gram Panchayat of Kusumi Block) of erstwhile Rairangpur Assembly constituency; the Hanuman temple of Nuru Badla (Mohanta Badla); Kalyan Mandap of Hatbadla, Durga Puja Pandals of Purunaghaty and Ichinda of Rairangpur town; Hara Parvati Pandal of Rairangpur to name a few.

There was a Shiva temple named 'Sri Khadakeswar Shiva Temple' in Rairangpur Bazaar constructed by the late Sri Gopal Chandra Ram, father of her political protégé Navin Kumar Ram which had fallen into disrepair over the years. She got it reconstructed by providing the local area development fund. Similarly, the construction of Banadurga temple in Badampahar, in the ancestral village of her in-laws, Tarini Temple near Women's college of Rairangpur were also rebuilt from the said fund.

She also facilitated the construction of the concrete road from Gandhi Park to the Railway crossing of Rairangpur which would always get washed away during rains.

Droupadi's contribution for the renovation and the construction of Jaher Garh, the place of worship of the Santhals was exemplary. Pradip Kumar Sahu, a party worker reminisces how the team members visited all Jaher Garhs to plant Sal saplings which is customary to the Sarana faith worship. She contributed for the barbed wire fencing and for the construction of the concrete roof top of the places of worship of all Jaher Garhs in the Kusumi block from the MLALAD funds. She distributed Himax solar lights to all the villages of the block. She also established community halls in all the Adivasi villages of her constituency. Soon after the end of the assembly sessions, she would visit her constituency and attend to the needs of the people of Rairangpur.

Her participation in the house for two consecutive terms spanning from the year 2000 to 2009 as a member in Odisha Legislative Assembly was outstanding.

Every year, three categories of awards viz. Pandit Nilakantha Samman, Utkal Gourab Madhusudan Samman, Utkalmani Gopabandhu Samman are given away to sitting legislators, former living legislators, and a junior member of Odisha Legislative Assembly respectively. According to 'The Orissa Best Legislator Award Rules, 2002', the award committee constituted by OLA considers the following aspects to select three outstanding legislators every year based on their, experience, attendance and duration of participation in the house, manners and behaviour in maintaining the decorum and dignity of the house, participation in debate and discussion, observance of rules and procedure, depth of knowledge on the subject presented, and contribution to various Committees of Odisha Legislative Assembly. Droupadi received Pandit Nilakantha Samman in the year 2005 for being the best legislator. As per the rules, the legislator getting Pandit Nilakantha Samman is felicitated with a cash prize of INR 1 lakh, silver replica of the building of Odisha Legislative Assembly, citation, and a shawl. Droupadi brought glory to the constituency by receiving the award.

Her contribution to ASECA is exemplary. As she was born and brought up in an Adivasi household, she was aware of the cultural heritage of Adivasis. She was also acquainted with the socio-economic challenges the tribals of eastern India encountered. These rich experiences helped her broaden her vision and contribute to the ASECA and the tribals. She would take part in various meetings of ASECA even before she was in active politics. She has helped in establishing many Jaher Garhs in her constituency where people having Sarana faith would worship. She would attend all the programmes organised by them. Along with these, her contribution for research, development, and promotion of the Chhau Dance (martial folk dance of Mayurbhanj) is exemplary. A detailed narrative on this will be found in the ensuing chapters.

Droupadi's enormous efforts for the inclusion of her mother tongue Santali in the Eighth schedule of the constitution is laudable. The Eighth Schedule of the Indian Constitution contains the list of languages that the Union of India recognises as official languages. There was a huge demand to include various languages as official languages of the nation. Under the stewardship of legendary Prime Minister Atal Bihari Vajpayee, the 92nd Constitutional Amendment Act, 2003 amended the Eighth Schedule of the Constitution to include Bodo, Dogri, Maithili and Santali languages. The bill was passed in both the houses on 22 December 2003. The President of India acceded to the bill on 7 January 2004, and it was gazetted on 8 January 2004. With this addition the total number of languages listed in the eighth schedule increased from 18 to 22. The original constitution had 14 languages. The then Deputy Prime Minister and Home Minister of India, Lal Krishna Advani introduced the bill. The bill was passed by the lower house of parliament (Lok Sabha) on 22 December 2003 and by the upper house of parliament (Rajya Sabha) on 23 December 2003. This was an ecstatic moment for all Santhals of the nation. Droupadi organised Santali Bhasha Divas for the first time on 22 December 2003 at Suchana Bhawan (now Jayadev Bhawan), Bhubaneswar.

Chief guest at Bamanghaty Mahotsav, Rairangpur in 2003, while being the Minister, Fisheries & Animal Resource Development, Government of Odisha

Jayadev Bhawan is a major convention centre adjacent to the Odisha state secretariat (renamed as Lok Seva Bhawan) in Bhubaneswar where several governmental and non-governmental programmes take place regularly. Droupadi delivered a speech in Santali in that concourse. There is also a Santhal women's organisation known as Rajgal Jaher Aayo Mahila Samiti. Delha Soren was the president, and she was thrilled to deliver the first public speech in her mother tongue Santali. Since then, every year on 22 December, Hassa (motherland) Bhasa (language) Vijay Divas is observed by the tribal fraternity to commemorate the official status given to their languages.

This landmark achievement of the inclusion of Santali as an official language in the eighth schedule of the Constitution also witnessed grand celebrations in Rairangpur under the aegis of ASECA, Odisha on 25 December 2003. Many eminent tribal leaders of the time who attended the concourse include Naran

Marndi, President, ASECA, Odisha; Sankha Hansdah, General Secretary, ASECA, Odisha; Droupadi Murmu, Sudam Marandi, Laxman Majhi, Braja Mohan Hansdah, Badha Besra, Lalmohan Baskey, Laxman Soren, Bhado Hansdah, Kanchu Charan Murmu, Paresh Chandra Murmu etc. Baripada, the district headquarters of the tribal dominated Mayurbhanj district of Odisha also witnessed magnificent celebration on 1 January 2004 as a gesture of gratitude to the Government of India and to recognise the contribution of the leaders who spearheaded the movement. It was a historic day indeed. A lot of research and development of the language has been made since then and Droupadi had also contributed to it in later years. In 2004, the centenary celebration of Guru Gomke Pandit Raghunath Murmu (18 May 1905 – 1 February 1982) was observed under the chairmanship of Droupadi. It saw tribal leaders irrespective of their political affiliations join in. She included and sought suggestions from senior leaders of the districts even though they were from different parties. Droupadi was gradually evolving as a visionary leader.

By the initiative of Droupadi and of a few other leaders, the place of worship for Santhals was inaugurated in the capital city Bhubaneswar by Government of Odisha in 2009 in the presence of Chief Minister Naveen Patnaik, veteran tribal leader Chaitanya Prasad Majhi, Minister ST & SC Development, Minorities and Backward Classes Welfare, Government of Odisha. A galaxy of eminent leaders attended the momentous event, namely, Biswa Bhushan Harichandan, Minister of Rural Development, Industries, Law; Surjya Narayan Patro, Minister of Information and Technology, Culture; Kanak Vardhan Singhdeo, Minister, Urban Development and Public Enterprise Golak Bihari Naik, Fisheries and Animal Resources Development, Textiles and Handloom; among others.

A 2500 square feet land in Niladri Vihar was earmarked to build a Jaher Garh which was inaugurated on 11 January 2009. Pandit Raghunath Murmu is the creator of the Ol Chiki script of Santali language. He is also known as Guru Gomke (the great teacher). Droupadi donated a life size statue of Guru Gomke Pandit Raghunath Murmu which was placed in the Jaher Garh at Bhubaneswar. The Santhal women's organisation Rajgal Jaher Aayo Mahila Samiti organised the event. Her old friends, Delha Soren was the president of the organisation whereas Priyamani Tudu was the secretary, Gayamani Besra was the director and Dangi Murmu was an executive member among others. All her friends as mentioned contributed to the cause of the cultural development of the Adivasis in the state. This historic feat by Droupadi to uphold tribal dignity was appreciated in all quarters. The Jaher Garh was used for celebrating Santhal festivals in the capital. One such festival called Baha Bhaga is observed before Holi on the 5th day after the new moon. A large congregation of Santhals gather every year to celebrate with new clothes, food, and festivities.

In addition to the development work during her two terms as MLA and Minister, she would take time out to spend time with the

Inauguration of Jaher Garh in Niladri Vihar, Bhubaneswar in presence of Naveen Patnaik, Chief Minister; Chaitanya Prasad Majhi, Minister ST & SC Development, Minorities and Backward Classes Welfare; Biswa Bhushan Harichandan, Minister of Rural Development, Industries, Law; Surjya Narayan Patro, Minister of Information and Technology, Culture; Kanak Vardhan Singhdeo, Minister, Urban Development and Public Enterprise Golak Bihari Naik, Fisheries and Animal Resources Development, Textiles and Handloom, and Droupadi Murmu, MLA, Rairangpur, 11.01.2009

students and former colleagues of Sri Aurobindo Integral Education and Research Centre, the school very close to her heart. Droupadi would attend a picnic organised by the school in the vicinity of the picturesque PWD bungalow of Rairangpur while she was a minister. She participated and helped in cooking as well. She attended picnics as a teacher in Suleipat dam and Ramatirtha river crocodile project near Jashipur. As a minister also, she would participate in the picnic with the same zeal. Humility coupled with dedication won her adulation from students, former colleagues, constituents, and people of the state.

Appreciating and celebrating cultural diversity is a winning personality trait of a great leader. Droupadi had an affinity for cultural diversity and honoured the multi-faith ambience in her constituency. Every year, Chhath Pooja is observed on the sixth day of the Hindu calender of Kartika Shukla paksha, six days after Deepavali. Mostly the people of Bihar, Jharkhand, Uttar Pradesh, West Bengal and a portion of Nepalese province worship the Chhathi Maiya, sister of Sun God and the form of Mother Divine on the auspicious day to offer gratitude for the abundance in the earth. There is a small Bihari diaspora in Rairangpur who have been living in the town for three generations. Jainandan Prasad, from the diaspora and protégé of Droupadi's husband recollected, "Droupadi didi would visit Rairangpur Chhath Puja celebration on the banks of Khadakhai river for more than two decades."

Rebati Giri and her husband Harihar Nanda were Droupadi's neighbours in her ancestral home in Uparbeda. Later, when Droupadi became Minister, she would often remember Rebati and enquire about her welfare. She would meet her family during village functions. Droupadi's younger son Sipun used to surprise them by visiting Rebati's home with sweets from Rairangpur and would have whatever they offered with love for lunch Sipun, though a son of a minister did not have any qualms in taking food in a poor household sitting on the floor. He would take rice, Bilati Poda (cuisine prepared by roasted tomatoes), Sukua (dried fish) etc. relishing every bite.

Tri-cycle distribution by Droupadi Murmu, MLA, Rairangpur, V.K. Pandian District collector, Mayurbhanj in Rairangpur on 15.10.2005

Rebati would say, Droupadi and her children did not practice discrimination based on the socio-economic status of people and would mingle very easily with everyone. Droupadi, her husband and children were frequent visitors to Uparbeda village.

In 2009, the General election and Odisha State Assembly election took place simultaneously. A big political change happened in the state before the election. There was a major political jolt inside the National Democratic Alliance prior to the election. The eleven-year long coalition of BJD-BJP split due to a disagreement on seat sharing in the ensuing elections. "Unfortunately, the seat-sharing discussions between the BJD and the BJP have failed. Therefore, we will go to the polls separately. The formula proposed by BJP is unacceptable to us" said Chief Minister and BJD party president Naveen Patnaik. His announcement came minutes after a last round of talks he had with BJP's Rajya Sabha Member of Parliament, Chandan Mitra, who had visited Bhubaneswar as special emissary of BJP's prime ministerial candidate Lal Krishna Advani. The final attempt to save the alliance failed when BJP rejected BJD's proposal for a lesser number of seats in both Lok Sabha and assembly segments, than the previous ratio of 4:3 between BJD and BJP respectively. After the BJP's dismal performance in Bhubaneswar, Cuttack and Baripada civic polls, the party's stock plummeted. Most BJD leaders were against maintaining the status quo in seat-sharing as the focus was on the winnability. The two parties of National Democratic Alliance had contested the Lok Sabha elections in 1998, 1999 and 2004, winning the majority seats and two assembly elections in 2000 and 2004, forming successive coalition governments for the two consecutive terms.

The political scenario took an altogether different shape in the wake of the BJD-BJP split with bickering, allegations and counter-allegations between them. The Hindu monk and Vishwa Hindu Parishad leader Swami Lakshmanananda Saraswati (c. 1926–23 August 2008) and four of his disciples were murdered on 23 August 2008 in Kandhamal, Odisha. It is believed that seven Christians and one Maoist leader indulged in the heinous crime on the night of *Srikrishna Janmastami,* the Hindu festival. This was followed by riots. Close on the heels of the incident, the villages were set ablaze. In general, political violence, religious intolerance and riots are not common occurrences in the peace-loving state of Odisha which practises Sri Jagannath culture and embraces all faiths with equanimity. These incidents shook 45 million Odias and their sentiments. A strong wave of Odia Asmita (Odia identity) sentiment of non-violence and compassion swept the state, and everybody expected the political leaders needed to retain the glory of the state. Odisha, the land of Lord Jagannath had always maintained the ethos of universal brotherhood, tolerance, compassion and above all the devotion to the Lord. Despite the BJD-BJP squabble, both the parties rose above their coalition differences to retain peace in the state. People of Kadhamal were living in camps because of the eruption of fresh violence.

The debates and dialogues inside and outside the assembly widened the rift between the allies. Senior BJD MP and former civil servant Pyarimohan Mohapatra was considered the prime political strategist of the time. The leaders of both the parties were at loggerheads over their understanding about Hindutva and secularism. Earlier to these incidents, the National Vice-President of BJP and former Union minister had also demanded that the party should withdraw support to the government in the wake of the killing of 12 tribals in police firing at Kalinga Nagar, Jajpur, Odisha on 2 January 2006. The Union Minister had also led a campaign against the Government of Odisha's move to allot the Khandadhar iron ore mines located in the horseshoe iron ore reserve of Northern Odisha to the South Korean steel major, Posco. There were quite a few ideological differences among these two allies over a period of eleven years. Chief Minister Naveen Patnaik who is a man of few words found it prudent and decent to part ways and contest elections independently. BJD and BJP announced their candidates and contested the next *Lok Sabha* and *Vidhan Sabha* polls separately. The decision proved to be favourable for BJD as the party won with a thumping majority in the Assembly Poll held along with the General election in 2009.

The 2009 Assembly election proved to be historic because of many reasons. BJD contested 129 seats out of 147 seats in the State Legislative Assembly and won 103 seats. It had polled an unprecedented 38.86 percent of valid votes in the state with 44.16 percent of the voting share in the seats it had contested. The figure was quite appreciable. At the national level, BJD had won fourteen Lok Sabha seats out of total seats of twenty-one. INC had won in six seats whereas CPI had won in one seat only. This was altogether an unfavourable election for the BJP which could garner only six assembly seats and no MP seat in the state. The BJD formed the Government under the Chief Minister of legendary Naveen Patnaik. In the centre, United Progressive Alliance with Indian National Congress as the biggest party came to power for the second consecutive time. This was not at all a good election year for BJP in the state of Odisha and the resolution to contest election separately did not prove tactical.

Droupadi with two consecutive assembly wins to her credit from Rairangpur (ST) Constituency was sure to go for a hat trick this time. Rairangpur did not elect the same person as the MLA from the same party for two consecutive terms. Earlier Haradeb Tiriya had won consecutively in 1952 and 1957 from Indian National Congress and as an independent candidate. Similarly, Arjun Majhi had won two consecutive terms in 1974 and 1977 from Utkal Congress and Janata Party respectively. Indian National Congress won two consecutive elections in 1980 and 1985 with Siddhalal Murmu and Bhabendranath Majhi as the candidates. Droupadi was the only candidate to win twice from the same party. She was also the only lady MLA from the constituency.

Droupadi was given a BJP party ticket to contest from Mayurbhanj Lok Sabha Constituency. This was also a gradual progression of her political career as she wanted to move to New Delhi to expand her range of service capabilities. The party leadership also supported her decision to contest the Lok Sabha election instead of contesting the *Vidhan Sabha* elections. Another candidate Jaduram Murmu was given the party ticket by BJP for contesting the *Vidhan Sabha* poll. This time the BJP could not retain the seat and came third in polling of votes. Shyam Charan Hansdah of Indian National Congress won the election getting 24,792 votes polling 21.53 percent of voting share. Purna Chandra Marndi of Jharkhand Mukti Morcha secured the second highest polling by getting 20,190 votes. Jaduram Murmu of BJP could garner 17,898 votes only with 15.54 percentage of voting share.

In the General Election, Laxman Tudu from BJD won the election as the member of parliament for Mayurbhanj constituency with 2,56,648 votes while Sudam Marndi of JMM polled 1,90,470 votes being the second highest. The third highest votes were polled by Droupadi Murmu with 1,50,827 votes and Laxman Majhi got 1,40,770 votes being fourth in the electoral race. The BJP could not win even one parliament seat out of 21 Lok Sabha seats in Odisha. This was Droupadi's first major electoral setback. Though she secured good votes in Rairangpur and was leading in the area, she garnered less votes in other areas of the MP constituency. This was a shock for her party men as well, who had always reposed their faith in her. The time to campaign for one of the largest constituencies was very short and she could not touch all cross sections of society. This was one of the lowest phases in her political life in the past thirteen years of her being in active politics. She tasted the face of defeat for the first time. Her party men got disheartened and most of them went into hibernation. The hustle bustle in her residence reduced to just a few visitors everyday. The change was very disturbing for her close circle of friends and family too. Many party men tried to analyse if it was a bad decision to contest for the MP election instead of the MLA without adequate preparation?

She used to visit all households, walking, in her MLA constituency. Such outreach did not happen due to lack of time. Many would taunt her saying, "where are all the people who would visit her?" Success has many friends of course. However, Droupadi was confident and composed as always. She knew that these situations were quite common in a democracy. Many popular leaders see defeats and become victorious periodically. These were not things which could shake her from inside. She was determined to work harder and be victorious in the next election.

Laxman Majhi, was a major political opponent who contested two Odisha state Assembly elections in 2000 and 2004 and one General election with her in 2009. Belonging to the same Santhal community with a very staunch affiliation for religious-cultural life of the community, Majhi had praised her grit and her contribution in the lives of Adivasis of the constituency. This speaks highly of her character. He never accused her of tampering or using any illegal ways to woo voters. He candidly said, that the election in a democracy, rests on the political weather, the performance of the party at state and at the national level etc. along with the popularity of the leader in the constituency. He had no complaints about accepting his defeat unlike other contemporary leaders.

After the defeat in the 2009 general election, Droupadi was staying in Rairangpur with her children and husband. Often Shyam Charan discussed her political contribution and the reasons for the debacle in the last election. A few political leaders of other parties were in touch with Shyam Charan for a possible opportunity for Droupadi to switch to another political party. She was offered a good party position and other resources by a major political party. She was however not interested in switching to any other political party after more than a decade of association with the BJP. The party had also given her a lot of opportunities and recognition as a leader. However, the pressure to decide was mounting. A reluctant Droupadi did share the information with her party protégé and workers. When they came to know about the offer, all of them denied for such a change as most of them including Navin Kumar Ram, and Sanjib Mohanty were working for the party since 1992 and did not want to leave their seniority and respect in the party cadre. However, they did not want to hold back Droupadi if she would like to join another political outfit as her personal choice. However, Droupadi said, "how can I do something which my supporters were not approving of." She turned down any such opportunities. Though Shyam Charan saw better opportunities for her in another party, he agreed with Droupadi's decision to continue to work for the party. Her ethics in politics and loyalty to the party is something very commendable and worth emulating. She and her co-workers have walked the extra mile to establish BJP in the state. And even though she was in BJP, she shared good rapport with other leaders of the state too.

She held many intra-party posts in the Bharatiya Janata Party, the biggest national political party of the time. She was the Secretary of all-India Women's ST Morcha of the party. She was the Party President twice for Mayurbhanj district and headed the Mahila Morcha (women wing) of the Western Mayurbhanj BJP too. She had also encouraged many women to lead. Whenever the need arose, she mentored an efficient successor to these posts.

Her contribution and dedication for the party has inspired many to follow in her footsteps.

Droupadi Murmu (sitting) with the women leaders of the Rairangpur town

Foundation stone laying ceremony of Rairangpur Women's College in presence of Jual Oram, Minister Tribal Affairs, Government of India and Droupadi Murmu, Minister, Department of Fisheries and Animal Resources Development, Government of Odisha on 11.02.2003

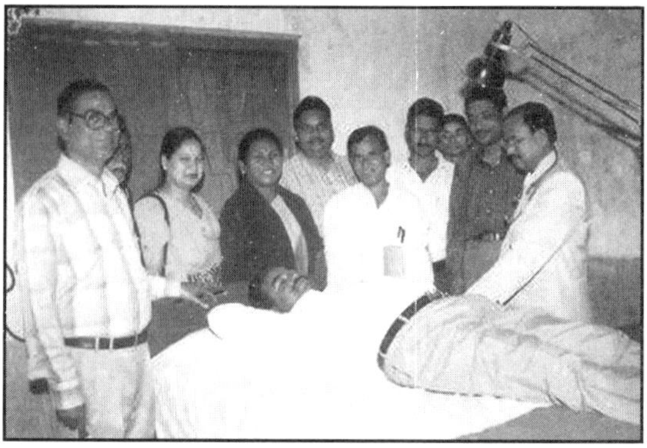

Visit to a Blood Donation Camp in 2004

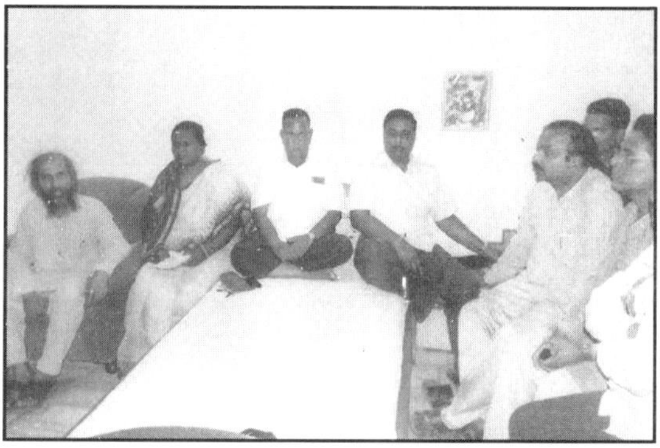

Hanuman Vatika dispute meeting with senior BJP leader Pratap Sarangi, Rabindra Nath Mohanta and Party Proteges of Rairangpur

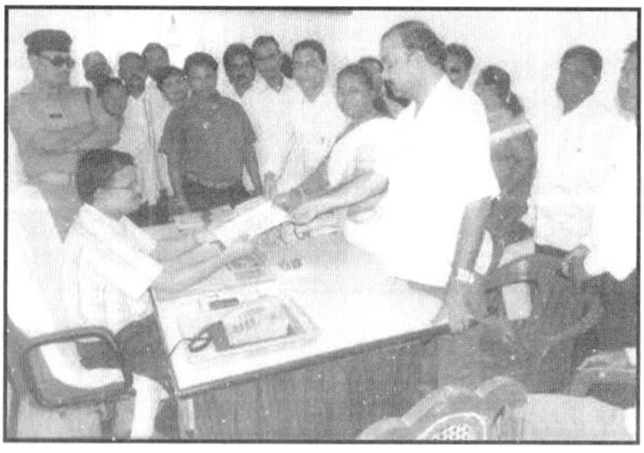

Nomination Filing on General Election of 2009 from Mayurbhanj Parliamentary Constituency

Speaking at the BJP Working Committee of Mayurbhanj at Rairangpur in 2004

Droupadi Murmu leading a Welcome Rally of K.V.Singh Deo, Odisha State President of BJP in Rairangpur

Pulling Chariot at Rath Yatra, Rairangpur

BJP Mahila Morcha Samabesh on the day of Gherao of Sub-Collector office, Rairangpur in 2005

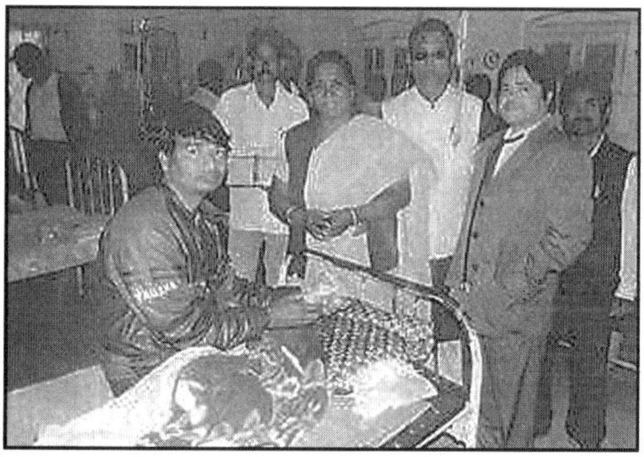

Distribution of fruits on the Vajpayee Jayanti in Sub-Division Hospital, Rairangpur along with Dr. Chhatish Chandra Mohanta

Non-residential Primary Teachers Training at A.G.Bai School, Rairangpur on 25.08.2005

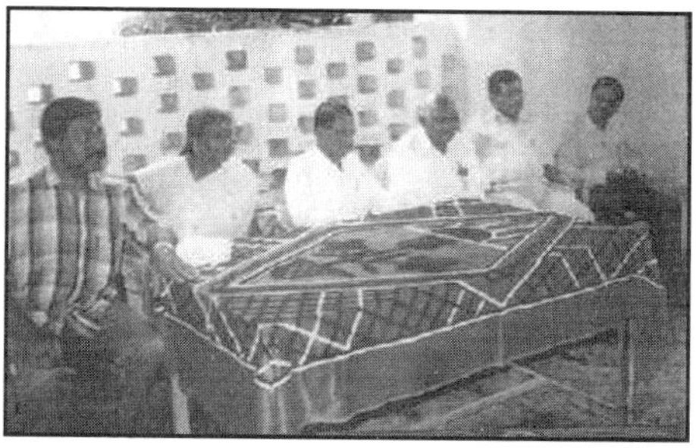

Chairman, Home Standing Committee, Department of Home, Government of Odisha during her second term as MLA

Attended as the guest of Sri Sri Ravi Shankar Vidya Mandir, Annual Day at Rairangpur in 2007

Chapter - 8

Tragedies and Triumphs (2010-15)

After the defeat in the 2009 General election for the election as the member of Parliament from Mayurbhanj, Droupadi was at her Rairangpur home engaged in regular public service. The party workers would regularly meet her to plan for people-connect alongside service projects despite the election result. Coincidentally, other parties were trying to woo her with alluring political positions. She decided to be loyal to her existing party and continued to work for the people staying in the BJP. Amidst all her hard work she had no inkling of the insurmountable turbulence and ephemeral rise that was in store for her.

Kumar Poornima or *Kumarotsav*, a festival of Odisha, was observed on 23 October 2010. In Bhubaneswar and Cuttack, *Kumarotsav* was celebrated with a good deal of festivities. Laxman (Lucky), Droupadi's son was residing in Bhubaneswar after completing his B.Tech. with his father and uncle. He was a good student. He went out to attend a feast with a few friends on 24 October 2010 and met with an accident. However, he and his friends hid the information from the family and said that he had just slipped, and it was a minor injury. On reaching home, Lucky complained of a headache. His father, uncle, and Satish Chandra Pratihari were also present. They could not fathom the intensity of his internal brain injury which was caused when Lucky had driven his motorcycle into a pole. His father advised him to take rest.

Next morning, he was serious and was immediately shifted to the hospital. Droupadi was in her constituency Rairangpur for few public programmes. On hearing the news, a teary eyed Droupadi ran to the place of Rabindra Nath Mohanta. As a doting mother, she was devastated on hearing the news of the hospitalization of her eldest son. She along with a few party workers immediately rushed to Bhubaneswar. However, it was too late to save Lucky as he succumbed to the head injuries and cerebral haemorrhage. Droupadi's second child and the eldest son had gone too soon at a young age of 26 years. It was a terrible shock and a blow not only for Droupadi and Shyam but also for their family and friends. Who would have ever imagined that Lucky, such a hale and hearty boy would meet such an end.

After Lucky's demise, Droupadi went into severe depression. Often, she would lock herself in the room crying in his memory and would not like to meet people. However, she had to meet people because she was in public life. She would go to Samadhi Mandir of the Divine mother of Sri Aurobindo Integral Education & Research Centre and Brahma Kumari's center in Rairangpur to meditate and get solace from the terrible grief of losing a young son. Most of the party members shared the shock and the grief.

On 9 January 2011, her nephew Dularam, son of her brother Bhagat (Pata) got married. The bride's name was Dulari, and it was an arranged marriage that was solemnized in the Haram Bariiyaat system in Droupadi's ancestral village Uparbeda. In Santhal families, marriages would span for 3-4 days. Shyam, Droupadi, Sipun and Iti would come every day from Rairangpur and spend the whole day in the village. In the evening, they would return. Dulari had studied up to class ten and Dularam, up to class twelve.

It was also time for the marriage of Droupadi's younger son Biranchi (Sipun). Sipun's marriage was solemnized with a bride from Pahadpur named Parbati Marandi on 8 March 2012 on the day of the Holi festival. It was a small gathering of near and dear ones. Sipun had eyesight challenges as he had impaired vision. However, he was very fond of traveling and watching village sports. He would also carry pictures of his family in his pocket. The photo album had become empty as he would misplace these pictures often after showing them to his friends. He loved spending time with friends even after his marriage. On one dark day, the 02nd of January 2013, a few months after his marriage, he went with a friend to watch a football match in Keonjhar by driving a motorcycle. This was new years' time and it was very cold in Mayurbhanj and Keonjhar districts of Odisha. Sports is a way of life in tribal parts of the country as well and winter is the best time to hold such sporting events. This is also a post-harvest time of festivities as *Makar Sankanti* was also in the offing. Sipun did not come back home on that day. The news of his accident came at around 9 PM spreading shock waves in the town. Droupadi ran to the house of Rabindra Nath Mohanta to seek help. Navin, Sunil, and a team of few friends rushed near Chadheibud jungle, Singada Chowk near Baitarani River bridge. The distance would be nearly 50 kilometres. They saw the motorcycle lying 400 meters away from Sipun's dead body. A heavy vehicle seemed to have crushed him as he was seemingly pasted in the road. This was unimaginably a horrific experience even to describe. The team took the body to the nearest Karanjia Sub-divisional hospital for the autopsy and on declaration of accidental death, brought the body to his Rairangpur home for cremation. The reason of death appeared mysterious. Here was a newlywed young man who went out to watch a match and did not return home. It was such a grief for all who knew the family. There were no words to console the bereaved family who had lost two young sons in a span of 28 months. Many investigations happened to know the cause of the death, and nothing could be found. It was more ironic that Sipun's last call from his cell phone was made to his mother. It was when someone was chasing him. The desperation of mother-son conversation was unimaginably tragic and helpless. There were many theories pertaining to Sipun's untimely accidental demise on a wintery evening in a jungle highway. The most believed theory about his death was that a few dacoits were chasing him as people recognised him as the son of a former minister. He was running along in the night and was probably hit by a heavy truck accidentally in the dark road as his eyesight was not good. His friend who he had parted from after the match did not have any clue as to what could have happened. No amount of reason could bring Droupadi's lost son back to life.

Sipun had died and his wife Parbati was in the family way. She lost her child in the womb due to shock, stress, and despair. Droupadi was very attached to Parbati and always treated her like her daughter. She wished to go back to her parental home, even though Droupadi was interested in her staying back. She wanted to treat her as her daughter. However, the shocked young wife of the deceased Sipun was in mental trauma and went back to her parents leaving Droupadi's home in Rairangpur. Droupadi was perplexed over the sequence of events taking place in her life. She was reminded of one teacher who described her as 'Sarvamsaha'. This would not have been proved by these tragic incidents. The Droupadi in Mahabharat had also lost her five sons in a day. She fell short of words to reciprocate as people poured in to give her solace. Words failed to describe the plight of an agonized mother who had lost three children in a row. The memory of the departed lives with her forever. Parbati opted to stay with her parents. Later, she had signed an agreement in presence of the village headman of Pahadpur and Kudarsahi that she would not come back to her in-laws.

Even when Droupadi had not come out of the absolute shock, her younger brother Bhagat Charan Tudu (Pata) passed away on 10 March 2013 within two months of Sipun's demise. Pata was suffering from cancer.

Droupadi was very fond of her mother Singo who would visit her often. And follow her like a shadow in all good and bad times. She too passed away after two months making a big void in her already shattered life. The loss of four dear family members was too much to take.

Soon, it was time for elections again. The general elections of the country and the Odisha Legislative Assembly election were declared at the same time in April 2014. Droupadi got the party ticket of BJP in Rairangpur assembly constituency. Though she was not prepared mentally, she honoured the party instruction. The elections were held in two phases. The results were declared on 16 May 2014. Though Droupadi could manage to garner 35506 (22.76%), she was defeated this time as well by Saiba Sushil Kumar Hansdah of BJD who received 51062 (32.72%) votes.

On the home front, Shyam could not take the demise of two sons and started falling ill very often. He was grief-stricken and neglected his health. He was admitted to a private hospital in Bhubaneswar. He had jaundice and non-stop diarrhoea. He was diagnosed with cirrhosis of the liver. His condition did not improve much even after adequate treatment. Shyam Charan was also complaining about the behaviour of the hospital staff as many friends visited to enquire about his health. When Delha came to see him, he cried inconsolably holding her hand. He knew that his days in the world were numbered. Maybe he was meeting her for the last time. They reminisce about the past when she was in AG Quarters quarter in Unit 4 of Bhubaneswar where Droupadi was staying with her and all the fond memories of the time they spent together. He used to be a regular visitor then to the place where Droupadi was staying and at the office of Accountant General in Bhubaneswar. Time had flown by so soon. The world has changed so much in three decades. Droupadi and her family decided to bring him back to Rairangpur.

A few days after returning to Rairangpur home, he had to be admitted to Rairangpur Sub Divisional hospital. Dr. Chhatish Chandra Mohanta, Medical Specialist and the son-in-law of her political mentor Rabindra Nath Mohanta was treating him. His belly swelled and his condition was deteriorating with every passing day. As a doting spouse, Droupadi sat in the hospital veranda clad in a green Jhela Saree with stripe work when her party proteges reached her in the hospital to meet him. Continued setbacks in the family had broken their financial security as well. Shyam Charan had left his bank job. He had no source of alternate income apart from the house rent and agriculture produce from his ancestral home. They had exhausted all the resources and found it constrained to treat him further. A few of her friends lent financial support and he was shifted to a private hospital in Jamshedpur, 68 kilometres away from Rairangpur. Possibly, he was destined to survive there for a day only. Next morning, he breathed his last in Jamshedpur on 1 August 2014. A stoic and grief stricken Droupadi was becoming lonelier as her life partner for 33 years departed from her life too. She was deeply in love with him ever since she knew him. It was very painful, an endless saga of agony and extreme panic, as one by one her loved ones were snatched away from her.

Statue of Shyam Charan Murmu in front of his ancestral home in Pahadpur, Badampahar, Bamanghaty Sub-Division, Mayurbhanj District, Odisha

The Samadhi (cemetery) of husband Shyam Charan Murmu & two sons Laxman & Sipun in the ancestral home turned SLS Memorial residential school in Pahadpur, Bamanghaty, Mayurbhanj

It is said that pain is inevitable, but suffering is optional. She decided to leave politics and dedicate her life as a full-time volunteer of a spiritual organization. She would go to village to do service work under the aegis of Prajapita Brahma Kumari Ishwariya Vishwa Vidyalaya popularly known as Brahma Kumaris. This international organization imparts socio-spiritual and educational teachings meant for personal transformation. The realization of the impermanence of life ushered in a lot of strength in her. Even though she had always known that spiritual knowledge helped to beat the odds of life, she could now implement these teachings in her personal life. Every soul comes to the world for a specific period and after the time is over has to go back. The soul has more freedom when it leaves the body. In fact, all in this world are free. The bondages are because of lack of understanding about the totality of life. This realization gave her a lot of strength to move on. It is also said that God is there for anyone who has nobody. The wisdom had helped her to brave the patriarchy she had to face in the absence of all male members of the family. Only with humility and emotional intelligence could she allow these encounters of personal losses to fuel her growth and spirituality. She was staying with her youngest daughter Itishree in Rairangpur. The mother and daughter duo beat all odds with a smile. Though success had many friends, these trying times could witness only a handful of family and friends who stood by her side.

Droupadi's youngest daughter Itishree had studied Intermediate in Arts from Ravenshaw University and bachelor's in arts from her mother's alma mater, Rama Devi Women's college (now a university). She then went to Pune to pursue MBA. She was also very polite like her mother and never let her friends realise that she was a daughter of a minister, recalls her friend Sthitipragya Biswal. She was staying with her friends in Sahid Nagar, Bhubaneswar to appear for various competitive examinations as well. They would go to have food in Sahid Nagar haat and lead a simple life. She would often think about her brothers and lament their early departure from her life. However, she faced all situations with courage, equanimity, and maturity despite her young age.

She qualified and joined as a bank officer in Uco Bank in 2013. After Shyam's demise there was only Droupadi at home when she came back from her office. Droupadi's brother Diku and sister-in-law Sakramani joined her to give company many times. The couple took care of Itishree as their own child as they do not have any biological offspring. Though this time period of four years was filled with great sorrows, there was a ray of hope in the household. Itishree's marriage was the silver lining in the four years of gloom and grief. She got married to an International Rugby player, Ganesh Hembram, Bachelor of Arts and bachelor's in physical education (B.P.Ed.). He was doing his master's in physical education (M.P.Ed.). He is also from Mayurbhanj and from the same Santhal community. He has four brothers. On 6 March 2015, their marriage was solemnized, and the family got a son in him. Though Itishree was not interested in marriage and wanted to take care of her mother, it was on Droupadi's insistence that she got married. With the passage of time, Droupadi came to accept Ganesh as her son.

Droupadi murmu's daughter Itishree with husband Ganesh

Mayurbhanj District Executive Meeting of BJP in Rairangpur, 2011

Chapter - 9

The People's Governor: Champion of the People (18 May 2015- 13 July 2021)

Jharkhand state was carved out from Bihar as the 28th state of India on 15 November 2000 by the Bihar Reorganisation Act. With approximately 32 various types of tribes, Jharkhand constitutes 26.3 percent of tribal population out of 3.2 crore people (2011 census) with the country's highest forest and woodland cover (29%), and largest mineral resources. Etymologically, Jharkhand also means the land of the forest.

On Monday, 18 May 2015 she was sworn in as the ninth Governor of one of the youngest states of the country. Hailing from the neighbouring state Odisha, the first state to be created on 1 April 1936 on linguistic basis, she was the first Odia lady to achieve this feat. She was also the first woman Governor of Jharkhand. The Chief of Jharkhand High Court, Justice Virendra Singh administered the oath of office to Droupadi Murmu. The then Jharkhand Chief Minister Raghubar Das, his cabinet colleagues, former Chief Ministers, Shibu Soren and Arjun Munda, Union Minister of State for Rural Development, Sudarshan Bhagat and a host of other dignitaries were present during the oath-taking ceremony at Birsa Mandap in Raj Bhavan, Ranchi. Ranchi is 196 kilometers from Rairangpur by road and Mayurbhanj is the northernmost district of Odisha bordering Jharkhand. Thus, there are several socio-cultural similarities among the tribals of Odisha's

Mayurbhanj, and Jharkhand's Singhbhum districts, in the language, festivals and lifestyle.

Taking oath as the Governor of Jharkhand in the state capital Ranchi on 18 .05.2015

Maiden visit of Governor Droupadi Murmu to her home town Rairangpur after assuming office as the Governor in 2015

Attending the Civic Reception organised by Rairangpur Municipality as the Governor of Jharkhand

Droupadi's appointment as the Governor of Jharkhand was sheer serendipity for her. A few months after the 2014 assembly election debacle, Droupadi Murmu met top leaders of the party and expressed her willingness to serve the nation. The words and opinion of a senior political leader seemed to have set into motion the prophetic rise of Draupadi Murmu when the top leadership of the country under the stewardship of the Prime Minister recommended her to hold the post of Governor of Jharkhand. Jharkhand with a sizable tribal population also received its first tribal Governor, after 15 years of its inception. Moreover, none of the Governors preceding her could complete a full term of five years. Droupadi Murmu had the privilege of adorning the highest office of the state for 6 years 55 days (18 May 2015 – 13 July 2021) making her the longest serving Governor of the state till date. This period also included the dreaded pandemic of the millennium - Covid 19.

The Part VI, Article 153 to 162 of the Constitution of Bharat discusses the roles and responsibilities of a Governor. Prabhat

Kumar (15 November 2000 – 3 February 2002) with a tenure of 1 year, 80 days was the first Governor of the state to hold office. He was succeeded by former civil servant V. C. Pande, from a family of civil servants of Rajasthan who was given additional charge as the Governor of Bihar. He stayed in office for a period of 160 days (4 February 2002 to 14 July 2002) only. He was succeeded by Justice Mandagadde Rama Jois from 15 July 2002 to 11 June 2003 for a period of 331 days. A former Indian police officer, Ved Prakash Marwah succeeded him for a period of 1 year and 180 days (12 June 2003 – 9 December 2004) only. He served as the Governor of Manipur and Mizoram as well. Syed Sibtey Razi served for a period of 4 years, 227 days from 10 December 2004 to 25 July 2009. He was a former political leader from Indian National Congress and the Governor of Assam. He was followed by Kateekal Sankaranarayanan who was in office only for 179 days (26 July 2009 to 21 January 2010) and former Chief Minister of Union territory of Puducherry, M.O. Hasan Farook Maricar for 1 year 224 days (22 January 2010 to 3 September 2011). Another leader of Indian National Congress Syed Ahmed succeeded him for a period of 3 years 255 days from 4 September 2011 to 17 May 2015. Thus, none of the Governors had been able to complete the full term of five years.

The first step Mahamahim Droupadi Murmu took after being sworn in as the Governor was to make the official residence of the Governor, Raj Bhavan, Ranchi accessible to the public. She also gave instructions to her staff not to deny access to anyone wishing to see her. She had advised the Raj Bhawan kitchen to practice vegetarianism. Vegetarian food without onion and garlic was served in the Raj Bhawan during her tenure. After the visit of Gurudev Sri Sri Ravi Shankar on 3 March 2017, one of the agriculture experts of the Art of Living started implementing chemical free organic cultivation methods in the Raj Bhawan gardens and farmlands which she wholeheartedly promoted. The Raj Bhawan also had a *gaushala* (cow shed) with a few indigenous cows and the cow dung was used as manure in the gardens. Chemical fertilizers were replaced by organic ones during her tenure. New varieties of plants and crops were tried in the garden on an experimental basis.

Often, she would visit the Rajendra Institute of Medical Sciences (RIMS), Ranchi, a state government run medical institute to help patients. As a Chief Guest on its first graduation ceremony on 18 October 2016, she emphasized the growing need of medical education to meet the demands of the poverty-stricken ailing people. She reiterated the importance of producing more health care professionals for the burgeoning need of the state and the nation. She also inspired the gathering to remain committed for the betterment of the institution embracing teamwork and goodwill. A leader is supposed to take care of the health care needs of the people. She lent a helping hand to many of her constituents, acquaintances to provide them better health care whenever she would be approached as part of her public responsibilities.

An annual discretionary fund of INR 50 Lakh is provided to every Governor of the country. During her tenure, 100 % usage of the discretionary grants was made through Direct Benefit Transfer (DBT) benefitting thousands of people of Jharkhand.

One day, Kamala, the wife of a rickshaw puller reached Raj Bhavan with her toddler child named 'Rudra'. She wanted to express her gratitude in person to the Governor for the benefits she received. On meeting, she mentioned that she was suffering from serious ailments and was not able to conceive. Empathising with her plight the Governor helped her get access to adequate help to give birth to a healthy baby.

As a Chancellor of the Government Universities, viz., Ranchi University, Ranchi; Vinoba Bhave University, Hazaribagh; Sido Kanhu Murmu University, Dumka; Birla Institute of Technology, Mesra, Ranchi; Birsa Agricultural University, Kanke, Ranchi; Nilamber Pitamber University, Medininagar, Palamu; Kolhan

University, Chaibasa; she focused on quality higher education of the state. She would call for a review meeting every quarter with all the stakeholders of the universities and would ensure that the examination calendar would be strictly followed. She provided minute personal attention to the recruitment of good faculty, upgradation of infrastructure, robust academics with favourable research ambience, and other related matters to ensure quality education to the students.

As the chancellor, she would also host annual convocations of the universities. One of the occasions was the grand 33rd Convocation of Ranchi University, the oldest university of Jharkhand on 30 September 2019. The then President Ram Nath Kovind presided over the convocation, also attended by the chief Minister of Jharkhand. President Kovind lauded Ranchi University for the fact that out of 56 gold medallists, 47 were girls. He motivated the students to become job creators, work in emerging technologies to their advantage, imbibe lessons from the glory of tribal leaders, and be steadfast to avoid bad influences like e-cigarettes. Inspiring graduating engineers in the 6th Convocation address of the National Institute of Technology, Jamshedpur on 20 March 2016, Murmu said, "Why should India remain a market? This is not acceptable. This is the reason why 'Make in India' was launched. I have come to you with a challenge - why not manufacture electronics goods in India? We have the talents, ideas and determination." While addressing the 10th Convocation Ceremony & Value Education Festival 2020 as the chief guest on 9 February 2020, organized by the education wing of the Brahma Kumaris at Mount Abu, Rajasthan, Bharat, she narrated how she practised the daily meditation and strictly followed the food routine of Brahmakumaris since 2009 and how she had benefited immensely from these. She inspired thousands of students, and teachers to bring about simple changes in their life with discipline and to inculcate human values, service, quality education, and nationalism.

Droupadi had envisioned a central tribal university in a place in Jharkhand which would be a tri-junction border of Odisha, Jharkhand, and West Bengal. The probable place would have been Ghatsila making it the second such university, the first being in Madhya Pradesh. Though the efforts did not yield immediate result, her vision would see the light of the day soon. The state government had taken initiatives to form the Jharkhand tribal university.

Her commitment to improved health care in the state of Jharkhand was also exemplary. Central Institute of Psychiatry (CIP), Kanke, Ranchi is a leading national institution for mental health in the country. Established on 17 May 1918, as the Ranchi European Lunatic Asylum, the centenarian institution is credited with many innovations in the field of mental health and neuro-sciences. Spread over picturesque 211 acres in the outskirts of Ranchi, CIP precedes many contemporary renowned Neuroscience and Psychiatrics institutions like NIMHANS, Bengaluru. The promising institute has been offering the latest medical advances in an ambience that promotes mental health and enhanced sense of wellbeing. The Governor had presided over the 100th Foundation Day of the institute providing yeomen service to humanity. She advised her principal secretary, Santosh Kumar Satpathy, IAS (2016-18) to prepare a project proposal for augmentation of the institution to an autonomous university and national centre of excellence. After a fortnight of brainstorming sessions with the concerned stakeholders, he came up with the detailed project proposal. Droupadi personally handed over the proposal to the prime minister and the president of Bharat as well. This project was very close to her heart. The initiative bore fruit and soon we might see her dream take concrete shape.

She has been a school teacher and therefore loved visiting schools to ensure continuance of quality education. Besides taking care of the universities, she visited more than 300 schools, especially Kasturba Gandhi Balika Vidyalayas (KGBVs) spanning over 24 districts of the state. She would invite the district collectors and superintendents of police for the possibility of developing infrastructure and security of the students. She also focused on the availability of scholarships, books and uniforms to scheduled tribe students. She ensured that these are provided to students on time and encouraged them to excel in studies. She would always emphasize the value of education. “Education is a vehicle through which transformation can happen of which I am a live example”, she would say.

She would visit orphanages and old age homes in the state and enquire about their welfare. The compassionate Governor would extend official help whatsoever needed from Raj Bhavan, and through the state government. Her heart would bleed for the countrymen who gave up their lives while safeguarding the welfare and security of the country. She would be present at the airport to receive the mortal remains of the martyrs from the armed forces of the Union and Police force to pay homage in their last journey.

Once there broke out a violent separatist movement called *Pathalgadi* in large tracts of tribal areas. It was mostly led by vested groups who wanted some sort of self-rule and they denied entry of government agencies to many villages. The Governor successfully intervened by making several rounds of deliberations with tribal leaders to resolve the conflict amicably. This led to sustainable peace and calm in the area.

One historic Amendment Bill was proposed by the government of Jharkhand under the stewardship of the Chief Minister on Chota Nagpur Tenancy (CNT) Act and Santhal Pargana Tenancy (SPT) Act. An approximate population of 3.4 million, ten percent of India’s tribal population reside in Chota Nagpur plateau. Santal Parganas has about 1,154,000 people. Half of the tribes belong to six large tribes of the country viz., Gond, Bhil, Santhal, Oraon, Mina, and Munda. The CNT Act came up in 1908 as a land law, then regarded as a protective shield for the land of tribals in Chota Nagpur. The SPT Act was a similar land Act for the Santhal

Pargana, brought about in 1949. These acts were formulated because many non-tribals had either duped or forced tribals to sell their lands at a cheap price. Both the Acts provide fullest protection to the land rights of scheduled tribes and make their land non-transferable to non-tribals. The state government wanted to amend the protective Act and proposed that the tribal land be made transferable for industrial purposes. According to the law-making procedure of the constitution, the state legislature after passing the bill sent it for the consent of the Governor. The Governor had reportedly received 192 objections against the CNT/SPT Amendment bills. She strongly felt that the amendments would be disastrous for the tribal communities and returned the bill without her signature with a query as to how the tribals would benefit from this. This stance was the result of umpteen discussions that she held with elected representatives and traditional tribal leaders. The Act never saw the light of the day. The media projected it as an ideological difference between the Governor and the Chief Minister, but this was not true.

During her tenure as the Governor, there was a change of Government in Jharkhand as the BJP Government under the stewardship of Chief Minister Raghubar Das was completing the five-year term in office. The assembly election for the 81-member state legislature was held from 30 November 2019 to 20 December 2019 when she was in office. The party or coalition needed 41 seats to form the Government. The BJP led Raghubar Das government with initiatives like 'Momentum Jharkhand' with 2.11 percent upward swing and more than 33 percent vote share could not retain the majority of seats while JMM with just 18.72% vote share could win 30 seats. INC with 13.88% vote share won 16 seats. Both JMM and INC with 46 members formed the Government. The BJP won in 25 constituencies but decided to sit as opposition. Hemant Soren, a tribal politician from JMM became the 11th Chief Minister of Jharkhand on 29 December 2019. Governor Draupadi Murmu administered the oath to the

Chief Minister and the council of Ministers. Thus JMM-INC rule began in Jharkhand. Hemant Soren had great respect for her and though she worked under different rules during her tenure, she had a good relationship with both the Governments which is indicative of her maturity.

When her school and college friends would visit Raj Bhawan in Ranchi, she would be extremely delighted and host them with open arms. She was always a people's person and loved to host visitors. Many of her friends, family members and juniors visited her during her six-year tenure as the Governor of Jharkhand. Her friend, Suchitra, Dangi, and Chuni recollect, she would tell her sister-in-law Sakramani to take care of her school friends in the Raj Bhavan who would be with them all the time they were in Ranchi. They would visit various scenic places of Jharkhand facilitated by her. One day during their stay in Raj Bhavan, they asked Sakramani that they would have Pakhala Bhat (watered rice)

Governor Droupadi Murmu with her school friend Chuni in Raj Bhawan, Ranchi

and Alu Bharta (mash potatoes) for lunch to reminisce about the olden days. On their return from touring for lunch, they found a feast of cuisines offered along with their desired dishes. Most of the cuisines fondly reminded them of their school days, especially the Matha Saga, a leafy cuisine prepared in Mayurbhanj district. Her school senior and roommate, Delha met her in Ranchi after many years. By then Delha had lost her husband and got emotional while speaking to Droupadi. Droupadi said, "let's not feel sorry about the past. People come to our lives for a specified amount of time and depart. We shall also leave the world one day. Let's not feel sorry about all the family we left behind."

Once during her visit to Rairangpur home, she came to hear about the challenges faced by the advocates of Rairangpur in justice delivery due to lack of library facility in Rairangpur Bar Association. Bibliophile Droupadi advised Akshay Kumar Mohanty, the President of Rairangpur Bar Association to provide her the list of books required for making a good library. On getting the list, she procured all the books in a month's time and advised him to take the delivery of a large volume of books worth more than Rs 3 lakhs. The Bar Association unanimously resolved to open a library for the advocates with the books gifted by her. This library was inaugurated in her august presence on 4 February 2021.

She would visit the Rath Yatra of Rairangpur every year during her tenure and pull the chariot of Lord Jagannath, Lord Balabhadra and Goddess Subhadra. Rairangpur Rath Yatra attracts a huge number of devotees during the week-long annual car festival. *Mela* (fair) and other amusements are held in the Block office field and adjoining area of the stadium for a fortnight. She visited the inauguration of many temples as well. One of these was the Shiva Temple in Sanpakhana village of Rairangpur constituency on 19 November 2009.

As the Governor, her first philanthropic venture was the formation of Shyam- Laxman - Sipun (SLS) Trust Board and a free residential high school in Pahadpur where her in-laws had their ancestral home. She would visit both Pahadpur and Uparbeda villages.

Many of her previous constituents from Rairangpur who would also visit Ranchi were offered hospitality in the Raj Bhawan. Surat Mohanta, Bikash Chandra Mohanta, Jaimuni Prasad Dash, S.S. Parihar and other functionaries of Raj Bhavan would render their services in various capacities. She would meet them irrespective of their affiliations. She hosted a team of probationer judges who qualified Odisha Judicial Service (OJS) in Raj Bhavan as one of the probationers was her constituent and granddaughter of Rasananda Lenka, renowned advocate of Rairangpur.

She would take every day as a new learning. Every day threw a new challenge at her and she faced it nonchalantly with her inimitable smile, grit and courage. The staff in Raj Bhavan, Ranchi included a number of officers and staff in the six years that she was in office. The two aide-de-camps had been drawn from the Military and Indian Police Service. Similarly, the Principal Secretary was a senior civil servant from the Indian Administrative Service. Apart from that, the Secretaries, House Controller, Officer-on Special Duty, Public Relations Officer, Photographer, security personnel, doctor, Personal assistants, cook, driver, gardener, etc. She left an indelible mark on them by her simplicity and frugality.

She completed her full term on 13 July 2021. A former BJP leader Ramesh Bais succeeded her as the 10th Governor of the state from 14 July 2021. He was also the 18th Governor of Tripura. Droupadi was seen off by a galaxy of leaders including the Chief Minister Hemant Soren and his family. The people of Jharkhand bid adieu to the people's governor with a heavy heart. She landed in Rairangpur stadium by the state chopper sent to drop her to her hometown. Rairangpur town received its leader with open arms. A public gathering of thousands of people across all cross sections of society were present to receive her in the stadium when she landed. She started staying in her Rairangpur home thereafter leading a simple life and dedicating her time to service. She especially took a lot of interest in SLS Residential school which provides free education to underprivileged students.

Welcome of Zilla Parishad members and Block chairman at her Rairangpur residence

Worshipping Lord Jagannath, Lord Balabhadra and Goddess Subhadra during Rath Yatra at Rairangpur

Performing Pooja to Lord Jagannath, Lord Balabhadra, and Goddess Subhadra in Rairangpur

Pratistha (Inauguration) of Shiv Mandir in Sanpakhna, Mayurbhanj on 19 .11. 2019

Chapter - 10

Generous Giver – Enlightening through Education (2016- 2022)

It was a momentous resolution when Droupadi Murmu committed to launch service projects in the fond memory of her loved ones who had had an untimely exit for their heavenly abode instead of just mourning for them. On the occasion of Utkal Divas and on the birthday of her late husband Shyam Charan Murmu i.e., 1st April 2016, she and a few of her family friends chose to launch a Trust with the objective of social service and upliftment of the community. Soon a philanthropic organization named 'Shyam- Laxman- Sipun (SLS) Trust Board' in the memory of the three dearest members of her family (deceased husband and two sons) was registered in Rairangpur. The objectives of the Trust ranged diverse subjects viz., development of ST, SC and other backward classes; organising of sports and cultural programmes in the village; boosting literacy; working in sync with government departments to augment the initiatives; providing vocational and livelihood skills to the local community; protecting and preserving forest and wildlife; empowering women by providing training on small savings, creating legal awareness, self-employment, health, education and family planning; development of slum children by introducing programmes on health, education, recreation, and nutrition etc. Most of the objectives had been framed by keeping a keen eye on the requirement of a tribal village.

In the same year, 2016, a residential school named SLS Memorial Residential School was set up in her in-law's village Pahadpur on their ancestral land. Pahadpur is a village in Talak Pokhari Panchayat in the Kusumi Block of Mayurbhanj district of Odisha which is 19 kilometres from Rairnagpur municipality. Anyone commuting from Rairnagpur, has to either travel to Kaduani Chhak or Jhaldunguri square to take a left turn to reach the village. The road from Kaduani square is nearer (7 km) to Pahadpur but it is a very narrow village road. The route from Jhaldunguri has wider roads and it is about 12 kilometres to the school. The mineral rich

Pahadpur: SLS Memorial Residential School & Ancestral home of Shyam Charan Murmu)

Badam Pahar village hosts the block office and has a rail connection. This is the same place from where iron ore is transported to Jamshedpur by Tata Steel Company for which he railway connectivity was primarily established.

Droupadi Murmu laid down her heart, soul and resources for the development of the SLS Memorial Residential school. She would visit this place during her tenure as the Governor of Jharkhand to spend time with the students and teachers to make sure that the school ran on the principles of imparting holistic education to children. She often speaks about the school passionately and expresses her stance of spending the rest of her life in service to humanity. The SLS Trust board and SLS Memorial Residential School Committee comprise of Itishree Murmu (President), Satish Chandra Pratihari (Vice-President), Janmejaya Giri (Secretary), Sumitra Pratihari (Cashier), Jagannath Murmu (Member), and Braja Mohan Murmu (Member).

There are ten qualified teachers who work day and night to ensure quality education in the residential school. They are Janmejaya Giri (Headmaster who is a retired teacher from Odisha State Government High School), Nigama Nanda Giri (B.Sc., B.Ed.), Menaka Tudu (B.A., CT.), Hemananda Giri (B.Sc., C.T.), Dumni Murmu (B.A., CT.), Rajendra Nath Giri (B.A., B.Ed.), Ram Chandra Marandi (M.Sc.Mathematics), Nilakantha Barik (B.A., B.Ed.), Sumitra Rout (Sastry in Sanskrit), and Narayan Hansdah (M.Com.). Some of the family members viz., Braja Mohan Murmu (nephew of her husband) and Biranchi Narayan Tudu (nephew) take care of the various aspects of the school.

The students and faculty members meditate daily in a hall separately earmarked for the purpose under the supervision of Dumni Murmu. Kalpana Mohanty taught music to students and Bandhu Sir taught classical dance forms, Adivasi dance, folk (Chhau) dance, and Jhumar dance to students. All three aspects of education - logic, music and meditation are practised in the school keeping in view the holistic development of students as advised by Gurudev Sri Sri Ravi Shankar also. Her stint as a teacher was greatly influenced by Sri Aurobindo's philosophy of education and therefore all five aspects of holistic education as envisioned by him were incorporated in the school curriculum.

Satish Chandra Pratihari (Muna), an old time protégé of Droupadi Murmu and her husband, takes care of all school matters. Menaka, the first teacher reminisces, that the school started with class six on 23 June 2016 (Thursday) with only nine students. Enrolling students at the school was a challenging task due to the lack of awareness about education in the remote village. In due course, people realized that it was a boon for underprivileged families. They reposed faith in the dedicated teachers who impart quality education in the school.

In the beginning of the pandemic, in 2020, the school had a total of 100 students. However, the student strength from sixth to tenth standard increased to 68 in the 2022-23 academic session. It used to be an Odia Medium School under the Board of Secondary Education (BSE), Odisha. In 2021, 15 students appeared in the Matriculation examination for the first time out of which 13 students passed in first division and two students got second division. In 2022, the school broke all records in the block and all the 20 students who appeared in the Matriculation Board examination came out with flying colours by securing first division with highest score of 83% by student, Damburudhar Giri (highest in block) and second highest score of 81% by Manmatha Mohanty.

Dharmaraj Marandi, a student of standard eight who was studying in an English medium school was unable to cope up with study pressure and left the school. When he was admitted to SLS Memorial Residential School, he could barely read any Odia alphabets. It was arduous for teachers to make him understand the subject. But the teachers took him under their wings. He got motivation to study for long hours beyond the school time. Since, the teachers and students live in one hostel, it was easier for him to get help from teachers all the time he needed. These joint efforts bore fruits and he passed the matriculation examination with 79%. His father was grateful and thanked the teachers profusely with teary eyes.

Hemananda Giri recalls that in 2016-17 many students who joined in class six could not even read the Odia and English alphabets properly. They had to be taught complex words in Odia through the timeless book '*Barnabodha*' (Odia books for alphabets and complex words). It's a stupendous achievement for the school that such students also secured the first division through sheer perseverance and grit thus ameliorating their standard forever. Had the students been left to their fate, they would never have had college education and would have ended up as drop outs!

A student is like a potential seed and the possibility of it becoming a gigantic tree is latent in it. Students can blossom to become limitless if they are nurtured well in the tender and formative years of their development. Many students from the village are now getting such opportunities to showcase their talents through proper guidance of the dedicated teachers. Encouraged by the adulation of the people and results, the school has plans to include classes in intermediate, and diploma levels so that quality vocational skills can be imparted to the socio economically backward children of the village and give them wings to soar high. The school has emerged as a beacon of light by providing value based holistic education to the children of marginalized and underprivileged sections of society and promises to change the lives of thousands in coming years.

The students are taught to value local culture and human values in the school. If an elderly guest lands up in the school, all the students bow down as a gesture of respect. These ancient values of Odisha might not be practiced in many modern schools these days. Bowing down to elders not only results in getting their blessings but strengthens relationships leading to greater happiness and contentment. Similarly, the very act of joining left and right hand to do Namaskar makes the *Ida* and *Pingala Naadi* meet each other, and the head is bowed in reverence to boost up the spiritual energy in the body.

The residential school serves vegetarian food served without onion and garlic prepared by many of Droupadi's extended family members. The nutritious *Sattvik* food helps students develop a pleasing personality. In 2022-23 the school had 68 students. Droupadi Murmu started these initiatives with her own personal resources. Often Droupadi's remuneration and daughter's salary would be utilised for these charitable ventures that she started. Though there are many philanthropists who are interested in working for the cause, the school committee is very choosy about taking help. Indian Oil Corporation Limited has tendered good support through its corporate social responsibility programme called 'Gyanodaya'. The school aims to expand by including skill education, technical education viz. diploma in engineering, and intermediate classes to name a few. The school intends to provide free education to many more students.

Along with free education to the needy, the SLS Trust board awards local talent every year. These awards recognise good work of the surrounding localities and accelerate the process of noble deeds through recognition and honour. Even through the Trust has been started with personal funds, a few philanthropic organizations have rendered help to add value to these philanthropic endeavours. These initiatives by the trust have gained appreciation in the district as well. The plans to expand the activities of the trust are on the cards in various verticals including skill development, education, entrepreneurship, and green energy too.

SLS Memorial Residential School Pahadpur, Mayurbhanj, Odisha

Launching the Philanthropic endeavours under the aegis of SLS Trust Board in 2018

Way to SLS Memorial Residential School, Pahadpur, Badampahar, Mayurbhanj, Odisha

Students in the class room of SLS Memorial Residential School, Odisha

Foundation of new building of SLS Memorial Residential School, Pahadpur,Bamanghaty, Mayurbhanj, Odhisha

Students playing in the SLS Memorial Residential School, Pahadpur

SLS Memorial Residential School Hostel in the ancestral home of Shyam Charan Murmu in Pahadpur, Badampahar, Mayurbhanj, Odisha

Droupadi's brother Tarinisen Tudu (Diku) with his wife Sakramani Tudu at Rairangpur residence

Felicitation meritorious students by SLS Trust Board, Rairangpur in 2018

SLS Trust Board hounouring meritorious student in memory of Droupadi's eldest son Laxman in 2018

Felicitation Sri Jagdish Mishra, Eminent Industrialist of Rairangpur under the aegis of SLS Trust Board in 2019

Chapter - 11

The Political Pivot: A Presidential Election that Propelled the Nation's Progress (The journey from India to Bharat) 2022- Continuing

In April 2022, the dream of Droupadi Murmu becoming the fifteenth President of India was mooted by a few of her party confidants in Rairangpur and they shared this possibility with few journalist friends. They perceived the apparent challenge which was to meet the mathematics of the Presidential Poll as the National Democratic Alliance (NDA) was falling short of 13000 value votes. Then the scattered imagination gathered winds and they calculated that if she became the candidate, the ruling Biju Janata Dal in Odisha, Jharkhand Mukti Morcha in Jharkhand and all the tribal Members of Parliament and Legislative Assemblies across the country would vote for her and thus the deficit would be met easily. The BJD in Odisha with 114 MLAs, 12 members in Lok Sabha and 9 members in Rajya Sabha aggregating a value vote of approximately 32000 was enough to bridge the deficit of votes needed for the victory of the NDA presidential candidate.

These thoughts took shape when a newspaper ran a story titled, 'Droupadi frontrunner in BJP's nomination race on April 30, 2022. The news spread in many states especially in Jharkhand and Odisha state media. She was the former governor in Jharkhand and daughter of the soil for Odisha and hence curiosity was evident. She was also very familiar to and friendly with the media of both the states and people were quite thrilled to witness this news. The news gathered unprecedented momentum and spread like wildfire. The whole country speculated about her candidature from NDA. This caught the immediate attention of the senior leadership of the party. The South Indian media also covered the news in May 2022. Thus, her non-controversial and self-less political legacy of 25 years in the tribal dominated areas of the country, prompted her well-wishers to dream big.

Soon, the senior leadership of the party started contacting her, adding fuel to the speculation. This course of events formed a strong backdrop as Bharat was yet to elect a tribal to the highest post of the nation, after more than seven decades of democracy. The successive governments in the union territories and states also have the onus to practise inclusive politics, based on constitutional values. Equal opportunity irrespective of religion, race, caste, gender or place of birth is one of the fundamental rights in Bharat and is the outcome of the long-standing struggle for political independence from the British colonial government. The citizens of the country have inherited a progressive and working Constitution even though it had more than hundred amendments in only seven decades of its existence.

Droupadi Murmu celebrated her 64th birthday in a simple way in her Rairangpur residence among family, friends and well-wishers who visited to wish her. In the evening of the next day, i.e., on 21 June 2022, which was observed as the International Day of Yoga worldwide, Droupadi got a call from the Prime Minister's Office (PMO). Bikash Mohanta, the former PA to Governor of Jharkhand, received the call and rushed to inform Droupadi. Soon she would receive another call from the PMO confirming her as the presidential candidate of the NDA. She was surprised when half an hour after the call, the media started highlighting the news.

More than a billion citizens of the biggest democracy of the world tuned in to their television and social media to watch the news.

People and media from far and near started pouring into her ward no. 2 residence in Rairangpur where she was residing after completion of her tenure as the Governor of Jharkhand in 2021 with her younger brother Taranisen and sister-in-law Sakramani. Tears of joy rolled down her eyes when she met her father figure Manoranjan Mohanty who she would address as Nandia bhai. They recalled the memory of the latter's best friend Rabindra Nath Mohanta. All the near and dear ones, who she lost in life flashed in her memory. These were the ones who would have rejoiced to witness this momentous resolution of the top leadership of the country. The list included her parents, husband, sons, brother Pata, mentors, and best friends who she would have shared the epic moment with. However, the whole country got ecstatic like never before. Her real-life story which was nothing short of reel life caught worldwide attention. All the fire that burns you turns you to glitter like gold.

Droupadi Murmu declared as the NDA Presidential candidate on 21.06.2022- First picture in the media

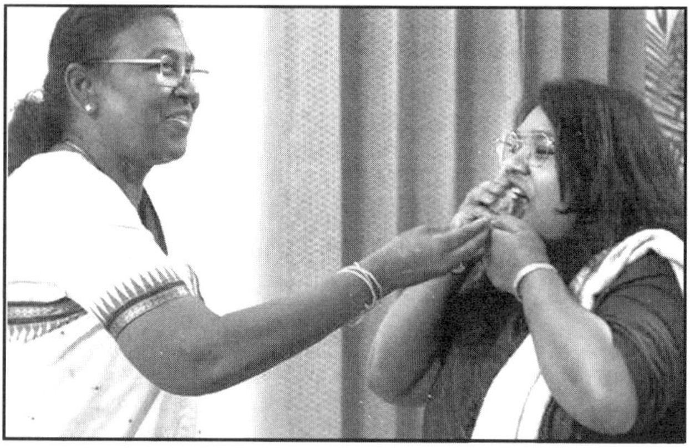

Mother–Daughter duo (Droupadi and Itishree) in New Delhi in June 2022

The media reached out to her teachers Bisweswar Mohanta, Basant Giri, and Basudeb Behera who live in Dubulabeda, Baliadhipa and Tentoposi villages respectively, adjacent to her ancestral village Uparbeda. They recollected their memories of more than half a century ago when she was studying in the village till class VII. They blessed her for a long and glorious life in service of her countrymen. Her school and college friends Tapati, Dangi, relatives Taranisen, Sakramani, Dulari, her political protégé, acquaintances etc. have also faced the spotlight and rekindled their olden days. The people of the town shared scores of pictures with her on social media. Soon the state police and central forces rushed to her place to manage thousands of people gathered in front of her residence to have a glimpse of their leader. It was a watershed moment not only in her life but in the life of the people of Rairangpur. After all, how many presidents of the country had they watched so closely and to whom they could speak with? This was an unprecedented historic occasion for everyone gathered there. It was nothing short of a 'tryst with destiny' moment for her and her acquaintances.

The euphoria continued for almost 16-17 hours at a stretch, till the next morning with meeting, greeting and non-stop photo sessions. No florist in the town was left with any flowers as flower bouquets heaped like a mountain in her home. The author connected Gurudev Sri Sri Ravi Shankar to her. He spoke to her from the USA and conveyed his good wishes. Many officials, associates, legislators of Mayurbhanj, constituents, and former staff of Raj Bhawan, Ranchi, met her to offer congratulatory messages. When she met Dr. P. S. Manikyeswari, former Sub-Divisional Medical Officer and one of the senior lady doctors of the Government hospital, both spent a few minutes of cordial time reminiscing the past while she was meeting thousands of people in person.

In the afternoon of 22 June 2022, Droupadi Murmu started off on her journey with two suitcases hurriedly packed by her daughter Itishree and cousin Dhani to leave for New Delhi enroute Bhubaneswar. People of Rairangpur were nostalgic of their association with her, reminiscing fond memories and simultaneously wondering when they could meet their leader next! The jubilation extended to Bhubaneswar as well. The party leaders, media, administrative officers, other acquaintances thronged to her guest house to have a glimpse of the future president on 22-23 June 2022 till her departure to the Biju Patnaik International Airport in Bhubaneswar. This destiny's child was all set to adorn the highest post of the country. History was ready to be scripted. The celebration continued throughout the country. Many newspaper articles covering inclusive politics featured the scheduled tribes which constituted 8.6 percent of the country's population. The constituent assembly had included all cross sections of the society and had representation from tribes too. However, there was no tribal lady in the constituent assembly. This move of NDA had fulfilled a long-standing dream of our forefathers to include the most marginalized section in the democratic process. The historic occasion became doubly symbolic as the country was celebrating 75th year of its political independence popularly known as *Azadi ka Amrit Mahotsav*. This master stroke by PM Modi had ushered a new era in Indian politics.

Droupadi Murmu sweeps the floor of Shiva Temple in Rairangpur ahead of her journey to New Delhi

Five years prior to this, in 2017, there was discussion on the presidential candidature of Drouapdi Murmu when she was serving as the Governor of Jharkhand. However, at that time, NDA chose a down to earth Dalit advocate, Ram Nath Kovind who was serving as the 26th Governor of Bihar. He became the second Dalit person to hold the post of the president of the nation after K.R. Narayanan.

There was an ocean of supporters, and admirers at the airport and the route she took in Bhubaneswar. Since she could not give any interview to the media, Itishree was requested in the airport to give a byte which she did candidly conveying that, her mother was a very simple woman who spent her leisure time reading books. She narrated how her mother made her way across the arduous path beginning from a remote village to education in Bhubaneswar to a career in teaching and her contribution in politics and serving people. She admitted that the news of being nominated as the NDA candidate for Presidential election was quite an unbelievable development for her and her mother as well. Navin Kumar Ram, Surat Mohanta, Itishree, her son-in-law Ganesh and two toddler granddaughters Adyashri and Nityashri accompanied her to New Delhi while she was preparing for her nomination. Union Minister of Education and Minister of Skill Development and Entrepreneurship and his aide organised all the logistics in a seamless manner, for her and the team.

On the occasion of Azadi ka Amrit Mahotsav, Bharat was destined to choose its fifteenth President in the sixteenth Presidential poll in 2022. On 9 June 2022, the Election Commission of India (ECI) vide notice no. ECI/PN/56/2022 notified that, according to article 62 of constitution of India, there is expiration of the term of the incumbent President Ram Nath Kovind and the necessary arrangements may be made to fill the post by 24 July 2022.

The citizens of Bharat, vote the representatives for local, state, and central government through fast past the post system by universal adult suffrage. This means, every vote has the value of 'one'. The total number of votes are counted to declare the victory and loss in the election that Bharat chooses its political representatives for three tiers of governance. However, the voting of the President of Bharat is not by the above-mentioned method of the fast past the post (FPTP). It is based on preferential voting through single transferable vote. According to Article 54, Part-V of the Constitution, the electoral college of the President of Bharat comprises of elected members of both the houses of Parliament, the elected members of the legislative assemblies of the states, and the elected members of the legislative assemblies of the Union Territories of National Capital territory, Delhi and Puducherry. However, the nominated members of the Parliament, state assemblies and state legislative councils in few states having bicameral legislatures are not eligible to participate in the election. Each vote of MLAs and MPs have a different value.

The total value of votes for all the MLAs for the 16th Presidential Election was 5,43,231. The total value of votes for all the elected MPs is 5,43,200. The sum for the value of vote of electors for the Presidential Election, 2022 is 10,86,431. For example, the value of votes of an MLA in Uttar Pradesh the most populous state of the nation has maximum value and is 208. However, the same for an MLA in Arunachal Pradesh is 8. There are two simple mathematical formulas to arrive at the value for the MLA and MP. An overview on the value of votes of MLAs and

MPs in the 2022 presidential election gives more clarity about the preferential voting adopted for the President of India.

Sl. No.	State/UT	MLAs	Population	Vote value	Total vote value
1.	Andhra Pradesh	175	43,502,708	248	43400
2.	Arunachal Pradesh	60	467,511	8	480
3.	Assam	126	14,625,152	116	14,616
4.	Bihar	243	42,126,236	173	42,039
5.	Chhattisgarh	90	11,637,494	129	11,610
6.	NCT Delhi	70	4,065,698	58	4,060
7.	Goa	40	795,120	20	800
8.	Gujarat	182	26,697,475	147	26,754
9.	Haryana	90	10,036,808	112	10,080
10.	Himachal Pradesh	68	3,460,434	51	3468
11.	Jharkhand	81	14,227,133	176	14,256
12.	Karnataka	224	29,299,014	131	29,344
13.	Kerala	140	21,347,375	152	21,280
14.	Madhya Pradesh	230	30,016,625	131	30,130
15.	Maharashtra	288	50,412,235	175	50,400
16.	Manipur	60	1,072,753	18	1,080
17.	Meghalaya	60	1,011,699	17	1,020
18.	Mizoram	40	332,390	8	320
19.	Nagaland	60	516,499	9	540
20.	Odisha	147	21,944,615	149	21,903
21.	UT of Puducherry	30	471,707	16	480
22.	Punjab	117	13,551,060	116	13,572
23.	Rajasthan	200	25,765,806	129	25,800
24.	Sikkim	32	209,843	7	224
25.	Tamil Nadu	234	41,199,168	176	41,184
26.	Telangana	119	43,502,708	148	17612
27.	Tripura	60	1,556,342	26	1,560
28.	Uttar Pradesh	403	83,849,905	208	83,824
29.	Uttarakhand	70	4,491,239	64	4,480
30.	West Bengal	294	44,312,011	151	44,394
	Total	**4,120**	**549,302,055**		**549,474**

The value of the vote of an MLA of the electoral college is calculated as follows:

$$\text{Value vote of an MLA in President of Bharat Election} = \frac{\text{Total population of state (1971 census)}}{\text{Total elected members of the State Legislative Assembly}} \times \frac{1}{1000}$$

The value of the vote of an MP in a presidential election is dependent on the number of elected members in legislative assemblies of 28 states and 2 union territories. Due to the absence of a legislative assembly in Jammu and Kashmir, the value of the vote of a Member of Parliament went down to 700 in 2022 from 708 in the 2017 presidential poll.

The mathematical formula to calculate the value vote of an MP is as follows:

$$\text{Value vote of a MP in President of Bharat Election} = \frac{\text{Total value of votes of all the MLAs of all states, NCT Delhi \& Union Territory of Puducherry}}{\text{Total members of elected members of Parliament}}$$

The total number of people's representatives in Lok Sabha and Rajya Sabha were 543 and 233 respectively totalling it to 776. So, the votes of MPs were 5,43,200. The total value of the votes of the members of the assemblies of all the 28 states and 2 UTs and the MPs, adds up to 10,86,431. That means in a presidential election, maximum votes of such value could be cast. The voting was held on 18 July 2022 as the tenure of earlier President Ram Nath Kovind's term was completing on 24 July 2022. Out of the electoral college consisting of 4796 MPs and MLAs in the list, over 99% cast their votes. The important misses include the member of Parliament of Gurudaspur constituency who was out of country for his treatment etc. The Union Finance Minister Nirmala Sitharaman and Union Power Minister RK Singh cast their votes wearing PPE kits as they were suffering from COVID-19.

The polling took place in 31 places which include Room no.: 63 of the Parliament houses and 30 assemblies of the states and UTs of the country. A total of 771 Members of Parliament entitled to vote (05 vacant) and similarly out of total 4025 Members of the

Legislative Assemblies entitled to vote (06 vacant and 02 disqualified) casted their votes. 100% voting by MLAs was reported from 11 states and one UT namely, Chhattisgarh, Goa, Gujarat, Himachal Pradesh, Kerala, Karnataka, Madhya Pradesh, Manipur, Mizoram, Puducherry, Sikkim and Tamil Nadu. She broke many records as well.

Droupadi Murmu has become Bharat's 15th President in the 16th Presidential election, and with that she would create history by becoming Bharat's first tribal President. Her total votes valued at 6,76,803, while her opponent. Yashwant Sinha could pull 3,80,177 votes only. Cross voting had become a political issue during the election as many people's representatives preferred to vote for Droupadi Murmu irrespective of the party's affiliation towards Sinha. As many as 17 MPs and 104 MLAs from the opposition camp had cross-voted for Murmu. The votes of 5 MPs were invalidated. A total of 4754 votes were polled, out of which 4701 were valid and 53 were invalid. The value of the vote for a candidate to be elected the President was 5,28,491. Droupadi Murmu secured 2,824 first preference votes, the value of which is 6,76,803. Similarly, 1,877 first preference votes were secured by Yashwant Sinha with a value of 3,80,177. As first preference votes secured by Droupadi Murmu were greater than the requisite quota, the Returning Officer, and Secretary General of Rajya Sabha declared her elected to the office of President of Bharat.

16th Presidential Election: NDA Presidential Candidate Drouapdi Murmu and UPA Presidential candidate Yashwant Sinha

According to Article 55 (3) of the Constitution, the election to the office of President of India is held in accordance with the system of proportional representation by means of the single transferable vote and the voting at such election is by secret ballot. According to the 84th Constitutional Amendment Act, 2001 population data from the 1971 census would be used till the occurrence of the first census after the year 2026. Thus, the value votes for the presidential election were calculated keeping the census data of 1971 as the reference.

Under Rule 40 of the Presidential and Vice-Presidential Elections Rules, 1974, the Election Commission of India (ECI) is required to maintain a list of members of the Electoral College. The list contains the names of elected members of the Rajya Sabha, Lok Sabha and the elected members of the Legislative Assemblies of States, NCT of Delhi and UT of Puducherry, in that order. Two members namely, Anant Kumar Singh and Mahendra Hari Dalvi were not eligible to vote in the election, owing to disqualification under Section 8 of R.P. Act, 1951 subsequent to the judgement of the competent court. Further, there were 5 vacancies in Rajya Sabha and 6 vacancies in State Legislative Assemblies. Therefore, there were a total of 4,796 electors in the electoral college for the sixteenth Presidential Election in 2022.

On 24 June 2022, she filed her nomination in presence of Narendra Modi, Prime Minister of Bharat, and other cabinet Ministers viz., Rajnath Singh, Amit Shah, Nitin Gadkari, many cabinet ministers, Chief Ministers from 12 states, other influential leaders etc. in the Parliament house. Her life depicted a sinusoidal curve with consistent crests and troughs. Just a week ago, she was leading a life like the person next door. Now, she was all over the media and the whole world was curious to know more about her personal and professional life. Who was Droupadi Murmu? What was her education? What happened to her husband and sons? Was her native village electrified? The questions were endless. Media thronged to Rairangpur, Uparbeda, Pahadpur residence with so much fervour that her kith and kin had no time to breathe. They were also rejoicing with the new normal that had happened in their life. The manager of SLS Memorial Residential School, Satish Chandra Pratihari, her brother's daughter-in-law Dulari Tudu, her brother and sister-in-law were all over in the print and electronic media.

Droupadi Murmu filing nomination for 16th Presidential Election along with Narendra Modi, Prime Minister, Bharat and other eminent leaders at New Delhi on 24.06.2022

One day before the declaration of her candidature, the opposition parties including INC, Trinamool Congress had declared former BJP leader and Minister Yashwant Sinha as the candidate. He filed his nomination on 27 July 2022. The last date of withdrawing nomination was 29 July 2022. 115 nomination papers by 94 individuals were received till 29 June, of which 107 were rejected for not meeting the required criteria. The nomination papers of Droupadi Murmu and Yashwant Sinha, four sets each, were found to fulfil all the requirements for valid nomination and were accepted.

Soon, she launched the nation-wide campaign by visiting the state assemblies and the leaders of the country accompanied by Union Minister of Jal Shakti among others. Her old-time personal assistant had also accompanied her. These trips were whirlwind tours in nature as they would visit almost two states in a day in a private jet. The states and UTs she had visited to campaign include Odisha, Bihar, Jharkhand, Andhra Pradesh, Tamil Nadu, Karnataka, Uttar Pradesh, Bihar, Assam, Sikkim, Madhya Pradesh, Chhattisgarh, West Bengal, UT of Puducherry, NCT Delhi, etc. Apart from Kerala, Telangana, and Andaman Nicobar Islands, she visited almost all parts of India in three weeks.

On 8 July 2022 when she visited her home state Odisha, she received greetings overwhelmingly. She felt nostalgic to go back to the Odisha Legislative Assembly where she was the MLA and Minister for two terms consecutively in 2000-2004 and 2004-2009. The legendary Chief Minister for the five consecutive governments in the state received her and invited her for lunch at his residence, Naveen Niwas. She was received by Chief Minister Naveen Patnaik and Union Minister Gajendra Singh Shekhawat was received by BJD MP Pinaki Mishra. The four had lunches comprising simple yet popular Odia delicacies in the cuisine namely *Baingan bhaja* (brinjal fry), Alu bharta (mash potatoes) and Badi chura (sun dried

Presidential candidate Droupadi Murmu having lunch with Naveen Patnaik, Chief Minister of Odisha at Naveen Nivas, Bhubaneswar, Odisha on 08.07.2022

lentil dumpling), etc. hit the headline of all the news channels on that day. In the Assembly, she mentioned Lord Jagannath and Goddess Subhadra to describe the camaraderie of Naveen Patnaik and her. This fellowship ushered a new era of politics of civility which Odisha loved to practise. Needless to say, he mentioned the same to the media after attending the swearing in function of the President on 25 July 2022 outside the Central Hall of Parliament.

In her home state Odisha, the BJD Party supremo Naveen Patnaik (who was like a brother to Droupadi) and Droupadi appealed to all the nine INC MLAs to vote for her as she was the daughter of the soil. The BJD MLAs had personally reached out to them. It is noteworthy to remind that Droupadi Murmu was a Minister in the coalition Government of BJD-BJP during 2000-2004. Naveen Patnaik held special affection for her simplicity and was the first one to tender his support even though he was on an official trip to Europe. This move won him a lot of accolades and promptly fulfilled the requisite value of votes Droupadi Murmu needed to win the election. However, it was historic that she got support from unexpected quarters. It seemed as if the Divine led her for a majestic victory with a record number of 64% valid votes to become the youngest President of the nation.

Apart from BJP, she received support of Biju Janata Dal (BJD), Janata Dal United (JDU), All India Anna Dravida Munnetra Kazhagam (AIADMK), Bahujan Samaj Party (BSP), Yuvajana Shramika Rythu Congress Party (YSRCP), Apna Dal Sonelal (ADS),Rashtriya Lok Janshakti Party (RLJP), Asom Gana Parishad (AGP), Paattali Makkal Katchi (PMK), Naga People's Front (NPF), National People's Party (NPP), Jannayak Janta Party (JJP), United People's Party Liberal (UPPL),Mizo National Front (MNF), Nirbal Indian Shoshit Hamara Aam Dal (NISHAD), Nationalist Progressive Democratic Party (NDPP), All Jharkhand Students Union (AJSU), Lok Janshakti Party (Ram Vilas), Maharashtra Navnirman Sena (MNS), Janta Congress Chhattisgarh (JCC), Sikkim Krantikari Morcha (SKM),Hindustani Awam Morcha

(HAM), Bodoland People's Front (BPF), Rashtriya Samaj Paksha (RASP), Jana Sena Party (JSP), All India Namathu Rajiyam Congress (AINRC), Haryana Lokhit Party (HLP), United Democratic Party (UDP), People's Democratic Front (PDF), Maharashtrawadi Gomantak Party (MGP), Hill State People's Democratic Party (HSPDP), Kuki People's Alliance (KPA), Republican Party of India Athawale (RPI-A), Tamil Maanila Congress Moopanar (TMC-M), Indigenious Peoples Front of Tripura (IPFT), Puratchi Bharatham Katchi (PBK). Shiromani Akali Dal (SAD), Telugu Desam Party (TDP), Jansatta Dal Loktantrik (JSDL), Shiv Sena (SHS) and Shiv Sena rebel group (Eknath Shinde). Jharkhand Mukti Morcha (JMM), Suheldev Bharatiya Samaj Party (SBSP), and Janata Dal Secular (JDS).

Even though JMM was in a coalition Government with INC in Jharkhand, it prioritised the tribal cause over politics. The JMM Party supremo, Disham Guru Sibu Soren wrote a letter to all the MLAs and MPs to vote for her. During her campaign, she met him to pay her obeisance. Chief Minister Hemant Soren's welcome with warmth for the erstwhile Governor of Jharkhand and NDA Presidential nominee, set a good precedent in politics of conscience. He is also a distant relative of Droupadi Murmu. Nevertheless, the decision was a big jolt to INC. Maharashtra was to repeat the footsteps of Jharkhand. The coalition Government of dissimilar post-poll alliance between Shiv Sena and INC was facing a crisis and found it tough to keep going. Eventually the partners parted ways leading to a bifurcation in Shiv Sena. The two warring groups of Shiv Sena supported her candidature in an interesting twist to the ongoing imbroglio of intra-party-political turmoil. Later a warring faction of Shiv Sena with leader Eknath Shinde and BJP led by Devendra Fadnavis formed the Government by taking oath on 30 June 2022 thus became the Chief Minister and Deputy Chief Minister respectively. She campaigned in Maharashtra to ensure their support as well.

Along with the Indian National Congress, the parties which supported her opponent Yashwant Sinha include, All India Trinamool Congress (AITC), Nationalist Congress Party (NCP), Dravida Munnetra Kazhagam (DMK), Communist Party of India Marxist (CPI-M), Communist Party of India (CPI), Telangana Rashtra Samithi (TRS), Samajwadi Party (SP), Rashtriya Janata Dal (RJD), Rashtriya Lok Dal (RLD), Communist Party of India Marxist–Leninist (CPI-ML), Kerala Congress Mani (KCM), Indian Union Muslim League (IUML), Jammu and Kashmir National Conference (JKNC), Viduthalai Chiruthaigal Katchi (VCK), Marumalarchi Dravida Munnetra Kazhagam (MDMK), Revolutionary Socialist Party (RSP), All India Majlis-E-Ittehadul Muslimeen (AIMIM), All India United Democratic Front (AIUDF), Raijor Dal (RD), Manithaneya Makkal Katchi (MMK), Kerala Congress (KC), Kongu Desa Makkal Katchi (KDMK), Kerala Congress Jacob (KCJ), Revolutionary Marxist Party of India (RMPI),. Congress (Secular) (CS), Janadhipathya Kerala Congress (JKC), Kerala Congress Balakrishna (KCB), Indian National League (INL), National Secular Conference (NSC), Nationalist Congress Kerala (NCK), Gorkha Janmukti Morcha (GJM), Tamizhaga Vazhvurimai Katchi (TVK), and Aam Aadmi Party (AAP).

One day before the election, political parties, and various organisations had offered prayers in the Sri Jagannath Temple at Puri, the Lingaraj Temple at Bhubaneswar, the Maa Samaleswari Temple at Sambalpur, the Maa Sarala Temple at Jagatsinghpur and other shrines across Odisha seeking blessings for a massive win for Droupadi Murmu in the presidential election. *Poojas (worship)* and *Havans* were conducted en masse in the state. In Rairangpur, Pooja was offered in the Lord Jagannath temple by the Bharatiya Janata Party workers followed by Prasad Sevan. The Brahmana Samaj and The Art of Living, Rairangpur did Havan (Hindu ritual where oblation is offered to fire) and Pooja (worship) in Punyeswar Shiva Temple, where she would offer sweeping services early morning every day after completion of her tenure as the Governor of Jharkhand. The Poojas were offered in the Bana Durga temple built by her in Badam Pahar, adjacent to the ancestral village of her in-laws. A huge number of villagers joined in the worship followed by Prasad Sevan as well. The worship continued throughout the country. These offerings created an unprecedented divine fervour throughout the nation.

Flawless security arrangements were made to ensure safe custody and smooth transportation of empty ballot boxes from Election Commission of India (ECI) to 28 States and 2 UTs on 12-13 July, 2022. Similar transport arrangements were made to bring back the 30 polled ballot boxes to the Parliament. All the ballot boxes and other election materials reached the Parliament House i.e., place of counting, by 19 July, 2022. The counting of votes took place on 21 July, 2022 at 1100 Hrs. Millions of people were glued to their television sets to witness this historic moment of democracy. Rairangpur's Droupadi Murmu was elected as the 15th president of India by defeating the only opposition candidate and a powerful political leader Yashwant Sinha.

With this, Droupadi Murmu became the first tribal Odia and the second woman to hold the position. She became the face of more than 104 million tribals of the country. Tribal music, group dance, attire and other cultural insignia would be displayed across the country mostly in eastern and central India. Odisha and Jharkhand topped in the list of celebrations as people of these states took pride to own her even though the whole country lauded her ascent to the top post. Women in the country also identified with her and celebrated with heart's content. School teachers celebrated as they felt that it was their victory. Her political rivals were also all praise for her. The Spiritual Organisations viz., Sri Aurobindo Society, Prajapita Brahmakumari Ishwariya Vishwavidyalaya, the Art of Living, and Swami Ramdev congratulated her. She was associated with all of them as she was a person of great spiritual affinity. People of Rairangpur feel privileged to have their place imprinted in the global map. Everyone in the country had a reason to rejoice as Bharat elected a president from the remote part of the country and from a seemingly marginalised section of society. The gigantic and enthralling moment was etched in the minds of millions who celebrated the victory as their own. They identified themselves with Droupadi Murmu and thus felt glorified by her elevation as the first citizen of the world's biggest democracy.

Good wishes started pouring in from far and wide, across the world to the supreme commander of the armed forces, the head of the country who could summon or prorogue the parliament, appoint the Chief Justice and the judges of Supreme Court and the High Court to name a few. Droupadi. Murmu was also the first President to be born after independence and was the youngest to hold the post. Prime Minister Narendra Modi along with BJP party president JP Nadda visited her temporary residence in Delhi to congratulate the leader. On 8 July 2022, senior BJP leader and former union minister Pratap Sarangi quoted that her nomination had brought glory to the constitution. The country could bring such pride by electing Droupadi Murmu to the highest office reinforcing the power of democratic values, breaking the myth that democracy is a game of the mighty and powerful.

The media persons across the country poured in to Rairangpur, and to her ancestral village Uparbeda, her in-laws place SLS Memorial School, Pahadpur, the Aurobindo Integral Education and Research Center at Rairangpur where she was a teacher. Her brother Taranisen, sister-in-law Sakramani, niece-in-law Dulari and a host of near and dear ones were all over television channels and other media, sharing their experiences. Her teachers, her students, her political protégé, her manager, her acquaintances, her constituents, her supporters, her rivals, and everyone who knew her, loved to share their experience with her in the media. Everyone who knew her spoke about her humility, goodness, quest for knowledge, her commitment to peace and vegetarianism, her spiritual interests, her patience, her belongingness, her resilience, grit, courage, and focus to make a better life for her and for her fellow beings and the community.

A girl, and a woman who was known to a handful for more than three decades of her life became one of the most searched persons on the internet. Her native village, which was not known to the majority of the world, became a historic place and everything associated with her changed forever. This is the power of democracy and dedication. People in the village and the city where she lived took pride in their nativity more than ever. A large quantity of sweets was distributed by the Biju Janata Dal, the Bharatiya Janata Party and other political and non-political organisations after the announcement of the results of the presidential election by the Election Commission of India. The non-stop bursting of fire-crackers which started from Bikash Medical Store was maintained and extended across the town. Bikash Medical Store is situated near Sri Aurobindo Integral Education & Research Centre in Rairangpur where her political career was planned every evening by her proteges. The whole town of Rairangpur where she spent most part of her life as a teacher, a legislator, and a political leader was decked in bright lights. The posters bearing her, Prime Minister Narendra Modi, and Chief Minister Naveen Patnaik appeared all over the town giving it a festive look like that of a car festival. The chariot of the car festival is also pulled in the same road every year where Droupadi would take part diligently. Every household was discussing, watching television, doing Pooja, distributing sweets and were engaged in things related to her elevation to the post of President of Bharat. Though Droupadi Murmu has fought and won many elections in Rairangpur, this election was exceptional as it was for the first citizen of the country. The euphoria, celebration and ecstasy carried on in myriad hues. Such incidents are rare in one's life span.

On 22 July 2022, a delegation of Padma awardees felicitated President-elect Droupadi Murmu on her triumph as the 15th and first tribal woman President of India. The names include Odia litterateur Padma Bhushan Pratibha Ray, eminent Santali litterateur Padma Shri Damayanti Beshra, Padma Shri Sabarmati, Lokakabi Padma Shri Haldhar Nag and Padma Shri Daitari Naik.

From 22-24 July 2022, the preparation for her entry to Rashtrapati Bhawan, New Delhi, the official residence of the President of Bharat had begun. The outgoing President Ram Nath Kovind had invited her along with her family for dinner. President Kovind, his wife, and his daughter received Droupadi Murmu and her family. Her daughter Itishree, son-in-law Ganesh and few of her close associates had the opportunity to dine with her. President Kovind's daughter offered her advice on how to conduct oneself as the president's daughter and how the President of the country is the nation's asset and *Raj Dharma* is supreme for her vis-a-vis her biological family. The next day, lunch with the Prime Minister and the team of Ministers took place. In the meantime, her brother and sister-in-law started their journey from Rairangpur to New Delhi via Bhubaneswar by carrying her favourite home-made *'Arisha Pitha'* (jaggery rice fried cakes). Many visitors from Rairangpur and Mayurbhanj districts gifted the traditional *Jhela Saree* for her.

At the swearing-in ceremony on 25 July 2022, forty-two fortunate souls from Mayurbhanj got an opportunity to witness the event in the Central Hall of Parliament with a seat capacity of 900 approximately. Her school friend Dangi Tudu described the event as if Lord Krishna had invited Sudama. She was one of the few people who were invited to the event from her school. Few others who could witness included Taranisen Tudu, Sakramani Tudu, Navin Kumar Ram, Sanjib Mohanty, Manoj Das, Bikash Chandra Mohanta, Ishan Mishra, Satish Chandra Pratihari, Prasanna Sahu, Naba Charan Majhi etc.

The oath-taking ceremony began with the arrival of the outgoing President Kovind along with Droupadi Murmu in a procession from the Rashtrapati Bhavan to the Parliament Building.

Dressed in a white Sonepuri Odisha handloom silk saree with green and red border, she epitomised simplicity and humility. She was escorted by Prime Minister Narendra Modi, Vice-President and Chairman of the Rajya Sabha M. Venkaiah Naidu and Lok Sabha Speaker Om Birla to the Central Hall of Parliament. As per the norm, she was administered the oath of office by the Chief Justice of India Justice N.V. Ramana. Along with the above union ministers, governors, chief ministers, President of the Indian National Congress, Sonia Gandhi, and a host of dignitaries etc. witnessed the momentous occasion. The oath of the highest office was pronounced in the national language Hindi, "I, Smt. Droupadi Murmu, do swear in the name of God that I shall faithfully execute the office of the President (or discharge the functions of the President) of India and will do best of my ability to preserve, protect, and defend the Constitution and the law and I shall devote myself to the service and well-being of the people of India". The country's new president was given a 21-gun salute after which she signed the oath amidst thunderous applause and thumping of desks by all the political leaders present to witness the historic event.

M. Venkaiah Naidu, Vice President of Bharat met the NDA Presidential candidate Droupadi Murmu at New Delhi

Excerpts of her presidential speech spoke volumes about her personality, her upbringing, her struggles, her resilience, lessons she received in Uparbeda and over all the glory of the great nation that traversed an arduous path of India to Bharat She reminded true to her roots when she posted "Johar! Namaskar!" (Johar mostly used by Santhals) as the first tweet on the official handle of Rashtrapati Bhavan after taking oath She emphasised how she started her education from one of the remote villages where getting education for girls was a dream. She had a meteoric rise from a ward councillor to a Minister to Governor and now as the President of Bharat by her consistent efforts and goodwill of others in the 25 years of her political journey. While being the school teacher in the Rairangpur Integral School for three years, the philosophy of Sri Aurobindo inspired her and she was greatly influenced by his ideologies on education. "My election is proof of the fact that the poor in India can have dreams and fulfil them too. It is a tribute to the power of our democracy that a daughter born in one of the poorest households in a tribal village can reach the highest constitutional position in India. That I attained the post of President is not my personal achievement, it is the achievement of every poor person in India,".

She also wished all the countrymen on the eve of Kargil Vijay Diwas which was observed on 26 July every year. She quoted from Santha Kabi of Odisha Shri Bhima Bhoi, *Mo jeevan pachhe narke padithau Jagata uddhara heu* (Let the world achieve salvation even if my life may be inglorious). The same couplet was also repeated by the Vice-President as well. Remembering the couplets of her school teacher Basudeb Behera she told, *Garib Bhi Sapna Dekhta Aur woh sapna pura hota hai* (A poor can dream and the dream gets fulfilled as well). She remembered her teacher's poem, *Dhana Nathile Kisa Hoiba, Manare achi Bala. Manara Bale Kari paremu Duniya talamala.* (Even though there is a lack of resources, I have the mental strength to move the world).

The prophetic predictions of Prabhakar Nanda in Uparbeda M.E. School proved correct after five decades. She rose to the highest position by being a *Sarvamsaha*. In Mahabharata,

Aswathama was instrumental in taking the lives of queen Droupadi's son. The 15th president of Bharat had also lost her two young sons in an untimely manner. These highs and lows seem to have been destined for her as well.

After the oath of office, Mahamahim Droupadi Murmu inspected the tri-services guard of honour at the forecourt of the Rashtrapati Bhavan. The Tri-Services Guard of Honour was also presented to the outgoing President Ram Nath Kovind at Rashtrapati Bhavan. Thus, history was created in the country, a candid demonstration of inclusive democracy. Dr. A.P.J. Abdul Kalam was named as the people's president. Droupadi Murmu was the president of the country from the marginalized section of society and can be named as 'President from the people'. Some opined that it was a master stroke to save the tribal vote bank, yet some others said she was an embodiment of women empowerment in modern India. Whatever the reason be, her elevation to the top post infused an unprecedented enthusiasm in rural Bharat which constitutes two third of the country's population and people across party affiliations liked her. She made her life worthy to adorn the top post beating all odds, braving personal trauma and societal stigma by showing exemplary resilience which made her a role model worth emulating. She is a true icon, and a role model which India must acknowledge.

Showing Honourable President Droupadi Murmu and Rashtrapati Bhavan, Raisina Hills, New Delhi, Bharat

Swearing in Ceremony of 15th President of Bharat

Tri-Services Guard of Honour for President Droupadi Murmu in Rashtrapati Bhavan, New Delhi on 25 July 2022

"The two opportunities Modi ji has received to choose a candidate for the highest office, he chose a Dalit and a tribal making his image stronger as a visionary leader," Amit Shah told in the release of the book, Modi@20 in a Bhubaneswar hotel on 8 August 2022. The whole nation had appreciated the intent of the Prime Minister to practise inclusivity during his tenure. This cascaded into multiple celebrations throughout the whole nation.

On August 27, 2022, the author along with a few of her acquaintances paid a visit to Rashtrapati Bhawan on an appointment to meet the President of India; they were overwhelmed by the hospitality while marveling at the intricate artwork. When it was their turn to meet, they found her as candid as always. She remained untouched even being the President of the largest democracy of the world. It reminded them about Chanakya Niti, 'नमन्ति फलिनो वृक्षा नमन्ति गुणिनो जनाः | शुष्ककाष्ठश्च मूर्खश्च न नमन्ति कदाचन || or '*Namanti phalino vrukshaah namanti gunino janaah. Shushka kaashthasya moorkhashchas na namanti kadaachan*' (A branch of a fruit bearing tree always bends down so knowledgeable persons possess humility. However, a dry log never bends, and a fool never shows respect to others.) When the author asked Mahamahim about her childhood and marriage photographs, she said that being from a humble origin, she did not have any barring one or two which might have been lost with the demise of her younger son as he was keeping those with him. She was very soft, nostalgic, and affectionate while conveying this. She reminded the author to correct the spelling of her name from 'Draupadi' to 'Droupadi' as there was an error in one of the spellings that she handed over pertaining to the book. When she handed over the editorial article that the author had written for a leading Odia daily that got published on 26 July 2022, she read it with interest making the moments more personal and heart-warming. Few other meetings followed. The most important one was on 4 February 2023 when she narrated very interesting facets of her life unknown to the world.

Every time the author meets her, it feels that she is truly a face of inclusive Indian democracy and a reflection of changing Bharat.

When the author visited her ancestral home in Uparbeda on 1 October 2022, her niece-in-law Dulari welcomed her and spoke

Sonia Gandhi, President of Indian National Congress congratulates President Droupadi Murmu in Rastrapati Bhawan, New Delhi in 2022

President Droupadi Murmu with Nirmala Sitharaman, Minister of Finance, Bharat in 2023

for a long-time reminiscing about the time when Droupadi would come regularly and sit in the veranda of her ancestral home, spend 2-3 hours during festivals etc. Rebati and a young neighbour Jitu Giri also talked about her contribution in the form of Kanhu River bridge, pucca roads from Kaduani to Uparbeda, the construction of Jaher Garhs, the construction of the boundary wall of Sindhu-keswar Shiva Temple, Livestock Aid Centre of Department of Fisheries and Animal Resource Development Odisha etc. Every person the author would meet to take inputs for the book, had a lot of pleasant memories to share.

A life worth living despite numerous challenges that were thrown at her from time to time, be it personal or political. She beat all odds and rose like a phoenix. Droupadi is a true inspiration to the new age Bharat. Basudeb Behera reminisced about the January 1975 event and said, "Had Biranchi Narayan been alive, I would have told him, your daughter adorned a bigger constitutional position than the charismatic former Prime Minister". The ambition of a father who aspired to see his daughter big after witnessing the massive public meeting of Prime Minister Indira Gandhi had been fulfilled. It made the country men feel so fortunate that the long journey from India to Bharat has been traversed in 75 years. This is a true and real reflection of inclusive democracy.

President Droupadi Murmu- A Reflection of Changing Bharat

Chapter - 12

Champion of Culture, Spiritual Seeker

A well-known *Subhasitam* (short educative Sanskrit verses containing truth in a condensed form) says,

'Sukhasya dukhasya na kopi data, paro dadātīti kubuddhiresha
Aham karomīti vrithābhimanah, swakarmasūtre grathito hi lokah'.

No one is responsible for our happiness or sorrows, but us. Since man is free to act, the responsibility for his actions lies solely with him.

It is depicted in the Ramayana that after the forest exile (*Vanvas*) of Ramachandra, Sita and Laxman, they were residing in the forest. It is described in the Ayodhyakand, when the king and younger brother Bharat reach their dwelling place with an army, Laxman thought that Bharat had come to wage a war against them. He conveys the news to Lord Rama. To which Ramachandra replies,

'Karma pradhān biswa kari rākhā, jo jas karaī so tas phala chākhā'

- Shri Ramcharitmanas, Ayodhyakaand 219:4

(Almighty has created the world and it is governed by the actions of the people residing here. Hence, as you sow, so shall you reap.)

Droupadi Murmu's life has been a delicate balance of non-chalance and gusto, a rare blend worth emulating by present-day leaders. As a *Karma Yogi*, she would welcome each day as it unfolded. Her journey of life fits well to a quote of American essayist **Ralph Waldo Emerson**, "Do not go where the path may lead, go instead where there is no path and leave a trail." She did not aspire to work in big cities. In fact, she left the government job at the capital city Bhubaneswar and chose to stay with her husband and children in smaller towns where her husband was posted as a bank officer. She has left an indelible mark in the minds of zillions by being attentive to the small things of life. She contributed to making her hometown, Rairangpur popular on the world map. She was happy to contribute wherever she got an opportunity in public life and blossomed like a lotus. In the scriptures, the lotus symbolises the ability to thrive under adversities by blossoming in murky water but remaining untouched by the mud. It signifies resilience, strength, purity, hope, resurgence. It is divine providence that she rose like a phoenix every time any personal and professional challenge threatened to decimate her. Perhaps the tumultuous journey of her life was meant to prepare her to adorn the position of the first citizen of the largest democracy of the world. Mahamahim Droupadi Murmu's *Sattvik Dhriti* (fortitude) is also reflected in her practice of vegetarianism. Her ascension to the highest post of the country has not only given the message of inclusive politics but has also emphasized on the personal character of a leader. Ethical political leadership is a mandatory value to be practised for long lasting of the democratic form of governance. One may consider these to be old fashioned, but in the long run, these human values of honesty and simplicity along with intelligence, pay dividends. She would mostly take a Jain diet which would be prepared without onion and garlic. She would sleep early and get up at the *Brahma muhurta*. *Brahma Muhurta* is that period of time which is the last part of the night which begins 96 minutes prior to sunrise and ends 48 minutes before the sunrise. Srimad Bhagavad Gita also emphasizes on moderation in food, rest and activity to be the path of Yoga.

> *"Yuktahara-viharasya yukta-cheshtasya karmasu*
> *yukta-svapnavabodhasya yogo bhavati duhkha-ha."*
>
> –*Bhagavat Gita 6.17*

(One who has regulated one's habit of eating, sleeping, recreation and work can mitigate all material pains by practicing Yoga.)

Gurudev Sri Sri Ravi Shankar also advises to conduct oneself in moderation and avoid extremes to be on the path of Yoga. He advises humanity to uplift the prana (life force energy) through awareness of food, sleep, breathing and meditative state of mind. Being in wisdom is very essential to eradicate the sorrows of the world as most of our pains arise out of ignorance. Droupadi Murmu was introduced to a number of spiritual organizations. In 2005, she was introduced to The Art of Living, founded by Gurudev Sri Sri Ravi Shankar. She (accompanied by Mamata Mohanta, school teacher and acquaintance) with her team attended the Rairangpur High school to participate in the six-day Basic course (Happiness Programme) offered by the organization. Ranjan Kumar Sahu imparted training on *Asana*, *Pranayam*, meditation, *Sudarshan Kriya*, and knowledge sessions etc. organized and assisted by Dr. P.S.Manikyeswari and the author (Dr. Vijaya Lakshmi Mohanty).

Later she helped in the enactment of Sri Sri University by hand holding the author of the book, who was the first volunteer and team member in the inception of Sri Sri University. The author would wait for her in the A.G. Square of Bhubaneswar and Droupadi would be glad to offer her a lift to visit the Assembly and the secretariat for the enactment of the first private university of the state of Odisha. The MoU of Sri Sri University was inked on 12 December 2006 during the BJD-BJP coalition Government in the state of Odisha. On 3 March 2017, during her tenure as the Governor of Jharkhand, Gurudev Sri Sri Ravi Shankar accepted her invitation to be a guest in the Raj Bhawan, Ranchi. The Hon'ble Governor also hosted a reception in honour of Gurudev at the Raj Bhawan. On her ascent to the position of President of India, he blessed her to emerge as a great president who the country will remember forever.

Droupadi Murmu's devotion to Lord Jagannath is also worth mentioning. She was a regular visitor to the Jagannath temple of Rairangpur. She had been a devotee ever since she had the Darshan of Lord Jagannath, Lord Balabhadra and Goddess Subhadra in Puri during her induction programme in Unit-2 Girls' High school, Bhubaneswar. After being active in public life, she would take part in the annual *Rath Yatra* (car festival) every year without fail. She would pull the chariot amidst the huge crowd gathered from far and near to be part of the grand event. This practice continued even after she assumed office as the Governor of Jharkhand in 2015. She continues to be a permanent invitee for the Rairangpur Rath Yatra committee. She was also the chairperson of the Rath Yatra committee of Rairangpur and discharged her duties diligently and judiciously drove governance there too.

On 22 June 2022, when she travelled to New Delhi after being nominated as the presidential candidate, she called Ravinder Nath Pradhan, Founder Member and Secretary of Shree Jagannath Temple, Shree Neelachala Seva Sangha, Green Park, Hauz Khas, New Delhi expressing her intent to have Darshan of the Lord. The Rath Yatra was observed during the transition time of her presidential candidature and her assuming office on 25 July 2022. Special security arrangements were made for her during the temple visit.

In her first visit to Odisha on 10 November 2022, after becoming the President of Bharat, she visited Puri to seek blessings from the Lord. Her historic visit and walking two kilometres in the *Bada Danda* (grand trunk road) to the temple amidst huge gatherings is etched in the memory of every Jagannath devotee. She was very emotional and raised her hands to surrender during the long walk. As per the custom, she took *Abhada* (Prasad or food offered to Lord) sitting on the ground along with her daughter and Dharmendra Pradhan, Union Minister of Education and Minister of Skill Development and Entrepreneurship and others. Jagannath *Sanskruti* (culture) is ingrained in every Odia, so also in her.

She is also a worshiper of Lord Shiva. The all-pervading Shiva consciousness would uplift her morale to serve more. During her tenure as an MLA and the Minister, she had facilitated in the construction and renovation of many Shiva temples in Rairangpur constituency. She has always participated in the Rudrabhishekam. She would sweep the Shiva temple premise of Punyeswar Mahadev temple in Ward no. 3 of Rairangpur every morning after completing her morning walk of more than two kilometres and would go back to her home quietly before dawn. She would do this without fail from the day she came back after completing her term as Governor, Jharkhand and before being nominated as the presidential candidate. The simple living of Droupadi has inspired many onlookers.

She is also a believer of the mother divine. She constructed the Bana Durga temple in the ancestral home of her in-laws in Badampahar. She has distributed many MLALAD funds for construction of temples, boundary walls of the Tarini Devi temple in her constituency. Needless to say, she has ingrained the values of Vaishnavism (Vishnu), Shaivism (Shiva), and Shaktism (Shakti).

Since Droupadi was a volunteer teacher in Sri Aurobindo Integral Education & Research Centre, she imbibed all the nuances of integral education and practiced the life skills teachings taught by Sri Aurobindo and Sri Maa. During her good and turbulent times, she was found visiting Samadhi Mandir situated in the school. She also practiced the Yoga techniques taught by spiritual Yog Guru Swami Ramdev under the aegis of Patanjali Yoga Kendra. However, her stint with Prajapita Brahma Kumaris Ishwariya Vishwa Vidyalaya (Brahma Kumaris) was longer as she would regularly visit the local centre to get solace from her personal trauma. She also visited villages as a volunteer of the organization. She accepted the norms and *Dinacharya* (routine) as advised by the organisation and followed this diligently. Her Rairangpur home and SLS school have reserved a space to practice meditation every day. All students and staff of SLS Trust memorial residential school follow the disciplined lifestyle for a healthy body, strong mind and balanced emotional health. She had benefited immensely from all the spiritual practices, diet, and *swadhyay* (self-study) she had done in her life. Droupadi has lived and breathed wisdom.

She has always nourished a nationalistic sentiment and believed that the Indian constitution has the power to safeguard the basic needs and provide security to every countryman, even to the most downtrodden. Her heart melted to see inmates having committed minor crimes languishing in jails due to lack of legal awareness and support. Some undertrials could not pursue the bail applications, while some others could not even afford the legal consultation. Some accused could not afford to pay the bail bond amount while some poor did not want to go out as food and shelter were available in jail. Further, shc cnvisaged that the social stigma led many accused to be disowned by their family members. These undertrials and convicts would find comfort inside the jail rather than trying to adapt to the outer world. She had a deep urge to help the underprivileged and appealed for the cause on various platforms. She wanted every citizen of the country to know about their fundamental rights and duties, as enshrined in the constitution, along with the preamble. It is her strong belief that these enable one to become a responsible citizen and contribute towards nation-building. *Desh Bhakti* (Patriotism) and *Daiva Bhakti* (Devotion towards Divine) are like two sides of the same coin.

Droupadi's cultural life is equally diverse, inclusive, and interesting. Every human being loves his / her cultural identity and has a deep attachment towards its development. It is no wonder that Droupadi Murmu is rooted to her cultural identity which she nurtured in her life.

Guru Gomke Pandit Raghunath Murmu has been a huge inspiration in her life. He was born on 5 May 1905 at Dandbose, a small village near Rairangpur town in Mayurbhanj district of Odisha. He was a school teacher. In 1925, he was serving as a headmaster in Badamtalia Model School when he invented a script for the Santali language with 30 alphabets, six vowels (*rahaalang*) and 24 consonants (*keched alang*). *Ol* means drawing an imaginary picture in mind without making any sound and *Chiki* signifies pictorial representation.

Once, Sachidananda Das, the Superintendent of Education of Odisha turned up for a surprise inspection and came to know that Raghunath Murmu had a hand press. The Ol-Chiki script received limelight for the first time in the state exhibition in February 1939 on Das's patronage. Subsequently, the Mayurbhanj Maharaja Pratap Chandra Bhanj Deo was briefed about the utility of the script. After long deliberations and discussions, he was convinced about its usage. He encouraged the Santhal people of Mayurbhanj to use the script to read and write their spoken language Santali. After three years, Pandit Murmu was transferred to Rairangpur High School on promotion. However, he resigned this government job in 1946 and devoted all his time for the development of *Ol-Chiki* in Santhal dominated states of India. He also published many books and journals in the Ol-Chiki script. The genesis of Ol Chiki script is interesting as its acceptance among people and Government through the efforts of many Santhal leaders and Droupadi Murmu.

Though many Adivasi cultural organizations existed, the first apolitical, social, cultural, and educational organization was formed in the name of Adibasi Socio-Educational and Cultural Association (ASECA) which got registered in June of 1964. Though it started in Rairangpur, Mayurbhanj, Odisha, ASECA has spread in eastern Indian states viz., Bihar, Jharkhand, West Bengal, and Assam. The efforts and movement was continued by the second-generation leaders after the demise of Guru Gomke Pandit Raghunath Murmu on 1 February 1982. The movement to include Santali in the list as the official language by including it in the Eighth schedule of Indian constitution gained momentum. Droupadi Murmu many Santhal leaders' dreams came true through the 92nd Constitutional Amendment Act, 2003. The Eighth Schedule of the Constitution not only included Santali but also Bodo, Dogri, Maithili as the official languages of the country. The Bill was passed by the lower house of parliament (Lok Sabha) and by the upper house of parliament (Rajya Sabha) and the President of India acceded to the bill on 7 January 2004 and it was finally gazetted on 8 January 2004.

It is said that motherland and mother tongue must be revered. Prakriti Kabi Gangadhar Meher had said in Odia, "*Matrubhumi Matrubhasa re mamata ja hrude janami nahin. Taku jadi gyani ganare ganiba agyani rahibe nahin.*" (Those who do not have affection towards motherland and mother tongue, if we consider them as knowledgeable, then there won't be anyone left who is ignorant). After the historic moment of inclusion of Santali as the official language, Droupadi organized Santali Bhasa Divas for the first time in Jayadev Bhawan, Bhubaneswar on 22 December 2003. With great enthusiasm, she delivered her speech in Santali. She was the Minister of state then. Every year *Santali Bhasa* Divas is observed to commemorate the glory bestowed to the language on its official status. She also patronized the Santhal Women's Organization called *Rajgal Jaher Aayo Mahila Samiti*. Many of her friends and acquaintances have been working for preservation, propagating the Santhal Asmita (Santhal identity).

She was also instrumental in construction of many Jaher Garhs, in Raiarngpur Constituency. In Bhubaneswar city, a Jaher Garh was established by the Government of Odisha on 11 January 2009. Droupadi had donated a life size statue of Guru Gomke Pandit Raghunath Murmu as a mark of respect. Though in later years, Guru Gomke's grandson contested the general election opposite to her, such political issues did not affect her faith and respect for Guru Gomke.

Her love for plants is worth a mention. She gifted plants to many of her friends and relatives when they visited her. She had also planted many Sal trees in Jaher Garhs. Indian society pays reverence to nature, viz., trees, birds, animals, mountain and water bodies as they believe them to be an extension of mother nature. The tribal faith's beliefs in nature are very evident and symbolic.

The demand of Santhals to include their mother tongue as the medium of instruction in academic institutions of Odisha dates back to the 1990s. On 25 February 1991, the Department of Education of Government of Odisha had passed a resolution to introduce Santali language in 30 primary schools of three districts of the state. Hence, 20 schools in Mayurbhanj, 5 in Keonjhar and 5 in Sundargarh got the opportunity to implement the same on a pilot project from May 1992. However, these initiatives did not yield a desirable response as students were more interested in learning Odia and English rather than Santali in school. Later, All Odisha Ol-Chiki Student Union (AOOSU) was formed at Rairangpur on 10 January 1999 with an objective to strengthen the movement for getting recognition of Ol-Chiki and its implementation in the educational institutions of Government of Odisha.

In later years, after Santali got official status, Santali literature got better recognition and schools in Santhal dominated locations got an opportunity to study the language. Jharkhand has recognised Santali as the second language of the state since 19 August 2005. Sidho Kanho Birsha University, Purulia, West Bengal; Ranchi University and some colleges of Jharkhand have been teaching the Santali language as one of the Modern Indian Languages (MIL). ASECA, Mayurbhanj, is providing bachelor's, master's and certificate programmes in Ol-Chiki. In certain education institutions this is an optional subject in BA and MA programmes. The Union Government included Santali Literature in the Union Public Service Commission (UPSC) examination as an optional subject.

A lot has been done by Draupadi Murmu and other Santhal leaders for the development of Chhau (Martial folk-dance form Mayurbhanj). Broadly Chhau dance is categorized into three types: Purulia Chhau, Saraikela Chhau, and Mayurbhanj Chhau. The first two forms use masks whereas Mayurbhanj does not. The music of Mayurbhanj Chhau is also different. The music that accompanies Mayurbhanj Chhau is *Bira baja* (martial music) while Jharkhand Chhau depicts socio-cultural stories etc.

As no mask is used in Mayurbhanj Chhau, the Bhangi and Mudra and a range of emotions can be expressed as per the demand of the chosen topic. Droupadi patronized the growth of Chhau which is basically an Adivasi folk dance. Her father was a musician in Chhau and her uncle was a make-up artist. She grew up watching these socio-cultural Chhau performances in her village. Mayurbhanj has 212 Chhau Organizations out of which Bamanghaty has 111. The interested youth artists of the village congregate to practice in the evenings. Thc Chhau Guru in the village teaches them dance forms of various characters. For example, if the *Abhimanyu Vadh* (the martyrdom of warrior Abhimanyu in Mahabharat) needed to be enacted, all the characters of the dance performance viz., Abhumanyu and Sapta Rathi (seven warriors) and their minute details of acting were guided by the Guru. The characters were drawn from the Mahabharat, the Ramayan and also contemporary social life. Being unable to sustain financial hardships, few Chhau Organizations have closed down.

In 1912, British King George V and Queen Mary visited India. The then Mayurbhanj king presented them a Chhau dance performance by 64 artists in Kolkata. This was published in many English magazines. Thus, Chhau gained popularity across the globe. In 1980, Dhirendra Patnaik of Rairangpur, Secretary, Odisha Sangeet Natak Academy, Bhubaneswar took local Chhau Artists for an International trip. They visited Funchal of Madeira Island, and Lisbon city of Portugal, Amsterdam and Rotterdam of Holland, a special dance festival of Spain, Rome, Bari and Milan of Italy. The next international sojourns of the Chhau troupe were conducted in 1985, 1989,1992 on invitation from France, British Council and Germany respectively.

Late Girish Chandra Mohanta, advocate and Sarala Samman Awardee for *Jhumar* folk music also contributed a good deal in organizing Chhau performances. He was the secretary of Bamanghaty Chhau Nrutya Pratisthan, Rairangpur from 1980. After his demise on 2 October 1998, Dusmanta Basa, office bearer with him since 1980 succeeded as the secretary. He has developed a curriculum for Chhau Education for North Odisha University (now Maharaja Sriram Chandra Bhanja Deo University or MSCB University), Baripada, Mayurbhanj, Odisha.

Droupadi continued to patronize Chhau Art from the year 2000 to place it in the cultural map of the world. She would visit the villages to be part of Chhau dance programmes held during the important festivals of the locality viz., *Chaitra Parva* (Spring festival), *Raja Parva*, and *Durga Pooja* to name a few.

Dusmanta Basa reminisces numerous instances of such programmes where Droupadi was invited as the chief guest and he as the keynote speaker. He is a connoisseur of the dance form for more than four decades and worked for its development locally as well as the rest of the world. Droupadi was instrumental in building the Chhau Bhawan in Kucheibudi, Rairangpur by allotting a special grant from the Chief Minister's special fund. This has given a lot of impetus to the research, training, seminars, and workshops of Chhau by inviting eminent Chhau Gurus of national and international repute. National Sangeet Natak Academy, New Delhi had provided financial support to train 32 youths in Chhau from 1994 to 2017 through a project under the tutelage of four renowned Chhau Gurus. Droupadi wished to start a regular training centre of Chhau at Rairangpur under the aegis of the Ministry of Culture, Government of India.

Every month, Droupadi was funding a stipend of her own to ten Chhau Gurus who were old and facing financial hardship. She would support dance troupes visiting various states of India to exhibit the Mayurbhanj Chhau in national festivals. Dusmanata

Basa escorted the artists to the National Festival in Nagaland, Joy International Festival, New Delhi, Dhauli Mahotsav (International Martial Arts Dance festival), Bhubaneswar etc. which were encouraged by her. After she assumed office as the Governor of Jharkhand, she gave support for the development of Chhau there as well.

Droupadi Murmu attending Chhau dance Programmes in Rairangpur

Mayurbhanj Chhau was displayed in Jharkhand National Festival at Sareikala and Jharkhand State festival at Silli, Ranchi. She would say, 'I belong to a Chhau family. I have been brought up watching Chhau in my home and would love to see it grow.' In olden times, Chhau was a popular form of entertainment in the villages. When the villagers would come home after all day's work, they would love to be entertained by watching Chhau dance among many other tribal dance forms. Chhau was the way of life in the tribal household.

The author's interaction with Droupadi Murmu dates back to two decades as she hails from the same town and a family acquaintance. The author happens to be her constituent as well. Droupadi calls the author's father Manoranjan Mohanty as Nandia Bhai (elder brother) and mother Dr. P.S.Manikyeswari as Bhauja (sister-in-law). Dr. P.S. Manikyeswari was also working in Rairangpur Sub Divisional Hospital for quite a long time and retired in 1999 as the Sub Divisional Medical Officer (SDMO) during her tenure as the Vice-Chairperson of Rairangpur NAC. Manoranjan Mohanty and late Rabindra Nath Mohanta, her political mentor, were very close friends from their childhood. Both would treat her as a younger sister and would help her every time she asked for personal and professional support. Tears of gratitude and happiness rolled from the eyes of Droupadi and Nandia Bhai when they met soon after her declaration as the presidential candidate at the former's Rairangpur home. This priceless moment was also captured by a few media persons who could reach her home. She greets the family with a lot of warmth every time she meets them.

When she was the Governor of Jharkhand, she would lend a helping hand to all visiting her irrespective of party affiliations. She would be present for all the invitations from the town as she considers them as a big family. On the *Ekadasaha* (11th day observance of the demise) of uncle Anil Kumar Mohanty, 6 February 2021, she came from Ranchi to console the bereaved family. She had hosted the author a number of times when she visited Ranchi to deliver lectures at Human Resource Development Centre (HRDC), Ranchi University. When the author visited for the first time, she sought permission before leaving the Raj Bhawan. Addressing her as the daughter of the soil, Mahamahim Droupadi Murmu ingenuously adjusted the saree of the author which left an indelible impression on her. The simplicity and affection had attracted many in the township to meet her and discuss issues of public interest.

During Makar Sankranti time in January 2022, the author visited her Rairangpur home with her student. She hosted them with hot, savoury, and customary *Arisa Pitha (jaggery rice cake)* which was being prepared by her sister-in-law Sakramani. Makar Sankranti is observed with all festivities in the locality where people meet their family and friends. Her humble countenance even after assuming important offices for years amazes many.

In the words of Droupadi Murmu, "*Bedana Madhumaya* (pain is pleasant) *Hahakaar Madhumaya* (despair is pleasant)". She has transformed all the challenges into opportunities for her exponential growth and contributed her might, skill, and time for nation building. Her narratives laced with a pinch of humour conveyed her magnanimity and wisdom. Bharat is maturing as a democracy and Droupadi's elevation to the top post in the 75th year of its political independence from colonial rule is quite momentous. Azadi ka Amrit Mahotsav year has witnessed an Adivasi woman in the position of the first citizen of the biggest democracy of the world. Mahamahim Droupadi Murmu is not just the embodiment virtues described earlier but a reflection of the changing Bharat.

Author Dr. Vijaya Lakshmi Mohanty presenting the books authored by Bhanumathi Narasimhan, sister of Gurudev Sri Sri Ravi Shankar to President of Bharat

At Rairangpur home soon after the declaration of NDA Presidential candidate with author Dr. Vijaya Lakshmi Mohanty and Manoranjan Mohanty (Nandia Bhai), father of the author, acquaintance on 21 June 2022

Bahadurga Temple in Badampahar constructed by Droupadi Murmu in Badampahar on 02.02.2009

Inspiring masses as Cultural Ambassador

Attending celebration at Rairangpur

CHAPTER - 13

DROUPADI MURMU: PEOPLE'S REFLECTIONS

BISWASWAR MOHANTA

Former Headmaster of Uparbeda M.E. School, Uparbeda, Bamanghaty, Mayurbhanj

I joined as an Assistant teacher in Uparbeda Middle English school in 1961. I went to Baripada from 1965 to 1967 for completing my study in CT (Certification for teachers) as per the requirement of the Government. In the year 1967, I became the Head Master in the same school. Droupadi took admission in the school in June 1968. She was calm, simple girl without any complexities. She was regular in class. She used to manage the class very well as a class monitor. She would raise her hand in case of even a small doubt and will not rest till she understands the lesson fully. In 1970, she passed class seven and was the first girl from the village to go for Higher Education to Bhubaneswar. She used to get a lot of prizes in the intra-school song, sports competitions. We thought she was a good student and would pass matriculation and could become a teacher in a school. We have never thought that she will be the president of the country one day. We are so proud of her.

BASANT GIRI

Former Teacher, Uparbeda U.P. School, Uparbeda, Bamanghaty, Mayurbhanj

Biranchi Narayan was a great philanthropist and contributed a lot to the development of both the U.P. & M.E. schools in Uparbeda. He helped in the growth of other organizations as well. Even then parents of the author of the book are great humanists of Rairangpur. Dr. P.S. Manikyeswari would give me physician samples every time I land up in Rairangpur for some illness. Nandia Bhai (Manoranjan Mohanty) supported me in many ways as well. The time when Draupadi got a school education was the golden age of education for teachers and students. There was so much respect for teachers. Parents, students, and teachers would stay in a straight line (Sarala Rekha) making the teaching-learning very pleasant and outcome-oriented. Though infrastructure developments have happened, the purity and transparency in teacher-student relationships are not seen nowadays. We need to bring back those values for the upliftment of education in society. Having said so, I bless Droupadi for a long and glorious life. May she be remembered forever.

BASUDEB BEHERA

Former Teacher, Uparbeda U.P. School, Uparbeda, Bamanghaty, Mayurbhanj

Biranchi Narayan Tudu, Droupadi's father, and a group of friends walked almost 20 kilometers on 22 January 1975 to attend a political meeting conducted by the then prime minister Indira Gandhi at the Bikash Nagar ground in Rairangpur. This was a few months before the proclamation of an internal emergency. Lakhs of people gathered to see the charismatic leader as she landed in a chopper at 9.30 AM. She spoke for two minutes in Santhali, one minute in Odia, and the rest of her speech she delivered in Hindi. People were amazed at her language skills. I knew that the MLA of Rairangpur had contributed to the Odia and Santhali part of her speech. I was also a part of the Uparbeda group though I was working in Nagbhan U.P. School those days. Biranchi Narayan was mesmerized and told that since she was the daughter of Prime Minister Jawaharlal Nehru, she could be so talented and was flying in the sky. Would this be possible for any woman in his household?

I am feeling nostalgic reminiscing about the epic moment of my life. Had he been alive, he would have seen that his daughter is holding an even bigger constitutional position and can fly across the globe to take part in various International issues. Only if he would have lived to see this! Prime Minister Narendra Modi's mother was so proud to see him. At least one of the parents would have been alive and felt proud of her.

LATE RABINDRA NATH MOHANTA

Former District President, Bharatiya Janata Party, Mayurbhanj

I would have been in Ranchi to witness the swearing in ceremony of Mahamahim Droupadi Murmu had my health condition been alright. I could not make it as my health did not permit it. It makes me very happy to see her elevation as the Hon'ble Governor, Jharkhand. I have been the witness to her victory and sorrow for more than two decades. (Excerpt of July 2015)

TAPATI MANDAL

Friend in Uparbeda U.P. School

Droupadi was a very good student. She would never gossip and waste time in useless pursuits. I have never seen her behaving rudely to anybody. She was calm and composed as a child as well. We took part in musical chairs, Pucchi khela, Kabaddi, and Jhilpi race sports competitions organized by the school under the guidance of our physical education teacher, Prabha Mohanta. She used to be the topper in education and a front-runner in sports. Our homes were very close by, and we would visit Tusu Mela together in Makar Sankranti. We would buy books and ink from Hatbadla (Badla) Haat. We did not have ball pens or fountain pens in those days. We would sharpen the bamboo sticks and make pens. Then we would dip the stick in an inkpot to write. My father was working in the Forest department of the state. I have two sisters and one brother. I got married very early after the completion of class five and have a son who works in Bengaluru. My husband, Lalbihari Mandal worked as an officer in a Tiles company in Musabani, East Singhbhum, Jharkhand. Now I live with my husband in Uparbeda after his retirement. I am also leading a relaxed life and spending time reading spiritual books, viz., Bhagawat Gita, Laxmi Purana, Surya Purana, Ganesh Purana, Padma Purana, Chittabodha etc. When Draupadi was a Minister in Odisha, she invited me by sending one of her aides to my place to sit beside her in a village meeting. She would always call me to come to her place and spend time. Due to my responsibilities as a homemaker, I could never go to meet her. On Draupadi's elevation as the President of India, I have given an interview to the media and wish to meet her and see Rashtrapati Bhawan.

MANORANJAN MOHANTY

Family Friend & Elder Brother

I have known Droupadi Murmu, the 15th President of India ever since she was a teacher in Sri Aurobindo Integral Education & Research Centre, Rairangpur in the neighbourhood of the late Rabindra Nath Mohanta, Advocate and the then district president, BJP and a well-wisher of Droupadi. Late Rabindra was my close friend, and my residence is also nearby. She used to visit Rabi often and he encouraged her entry into politics. She was a councilor of Rairangpur NAC and was Vice-Chairperson as well. Later on, she contested the Assembly elections to become an MLA twice from Rairangpur (ST) Constituency. She was made a Minister as well and earned name and fame with her performance. Further, she went on to become the Governor of Jharkhand.

And presently, she is donning the position of the first citizen of the nation. She is my younger sister full of reverence for me. She has visited us on many occasions and stood by our side when we needed it. I can never forget her visit to my residence to attend the last rites of my late younger brother while being the Governor of Jharkhand. After completion of the tenure as the Governor, she continued visiting our acquaintances. As an elder brother, I wish her an eventful tenure and a long, healthy life to emerge as a great President of the nation.

DANGI MURMU

Chief Accounts Officer (Ret'd), Central Excise, Customs and Service Tax (now GST, Central Excise and Customs), Bhubaneswar, Odisha, Droupadi's best friend, Unit 2 Girls High School, Bhubaneswar, Odisha

I am from Mayurbhanj and Droupadi and I were great friends while in the Unit 2 Girls' High School. My father Bhagabat Murmu was like a kingmaker and worked with all eminent tribal leaders of the Bamanghaty sub-division of the time. He was a freedom fighter as well who was jailed for participating in India's political independence.

During our student life, we would go to meet many leaders with him. Droupadi's patience is unparalleled. We have just one photograph from our school days. When we were passing out of school in class eleven, we framed our memory in a picture where Droupadi, Sumitra Kisku, and I were there. That was the only picture Droupadi had of her school days with friends. We became very fast friends in school and always remained in touch. My family was with her family in good and bad times.

DELHA SOREN

College Senior and Family Friend

Droupadi has gifted me the flowering plant that is there in front of my Bhubaneswar home.

Droupadi would love to come to my place and have food whenever she had some time while in

Bhubaneswar. I also head Santhal women's organization known as Rajgal Jaher Aayo Mahila Samiti as the president. Every year on 22 December, we observe the Santali Bhasa Divas to commemorate the official status of Santali by its inclusion in the 8th Schedule of the Constitution of Bharat. This is also very close to Droupadi's heart.

PROF. (DR.) ARCHITA PATNAIK

Professor, Department of Chemistry
Indian Institute of Technology (IIT), Madras
(School friend in Unit 2 Girls' High School, Bhubaneswar)

Thinking today, it feels gratifying and blessed about life's phases, starting from the very stage of germination in the late sixties and early seventies. The academic and cultural conditioning in my school (Capital Girls High School, Unit 2, Bhubaneswar) has instilled wisdom and knowledge, eclipsing my own and the expectations of my teachers. Here, in this school comes Ms. Droupadi who joined class 8th, section B in 1970. I mostly missed her those days since I was in section A. Nevertheless, with the blessed school and family in their background, she was extremely meticulous in developing the physical, mental, societal, and spiritual quotients of her personality to face the world with a strong belief that 'she can'. 'Raw was Receptive': those formative years with child-like simplicity have provided her the capacity to absorb and give back immensely with reverence to all. Today while witnessing her life's progression, I realize that we never know the circles of our lives; what is expected of us is true surrender and sincere work to the cause we are given. Droupadi has realized that living life's not about our day-to- day affairs, it is about understanding and discovering our true nature, our true self—which is Perfect and Limitless. During her first visit to Odisha after becoming the president of India, her devotion and unreserved surrender to Lord Jagannath with both hands skywards while walking a 2 kilometers distance to the main entrance of the temple captivated every conscious human on this earth. Her revealing confidence and execution of duties vested in her are a joy to behold. Her advancement is not accidental, it is her pursuit of recognizing the value system and delivering on those values. I wish her glory while she takes India to a greater height.

DR. P.S. MANIKYESWARI

Former Sub-Divisional Medical Officer, Rairangpur, Family Friend

The fifteenth president of India, Mahamahim Droupadi Murmu's life has been incredible- especially the journey from a simple village girl to the topmost position in the country. She has just risen like a phoenix from the ashes of her personal woes and tragedies, and with her perseverance, tenacity, and grit, sailed through the ocean of tears, and braving the rough weather, paved a path to success and position.

From the councilor of a notified area council to adorning the post of minister twice in different portfolios to the governor, then on to reaching the coveted post of president of the biggest democracy in the world is not just a cakewalk for her but makes indeed an altogether unique success story. The most appealing and adorable aspects of her personality are her simplicity, humility, and camaraderie.

I was working as a medical officer (used to be a lady assistant surgeon those days) in Rairangpur hospital, when she was a young school-going girl (the year 1966). She was born a philanthropist. She has been a close family friend of ours all these years. She visited us on many occasions when she was minister and governor. She would grace us with her presence whenever we needed it. She never ever shows off her position or power. I wish her a very successful and eventful tenure as president. I wish her a long and healthy life.

BIKASH MOHANTA

Former Personal Assistant to the Governor Jharkhand

My journey with Mahamahim Droupadi Murmu has been incredible. Droupadi didi's family and my family have been associated with each other for more than three decades. There have been numerous political and personal events in these years which we witnessed together. She has been a kind, compassionate, and guileless human being dedicated to social service. Volumes can be written on her. Her respect for elders is praiseworthy. She would take input from everyone while making a decision for the organization, which made her a much-adored mass leader. I had the opportunity to work with her as the Personal Assistant while she was the Governor of Jharkhand. As a Governor of Jharkhand, she did not miss any opportunity to serve the people. This made her truly a 'People's Governor'.

NAVIN KUMAR RAM

Secretary of Odisha State, Former District President of Mayurbhanj, Bharatiya Janata Party, Political Protégé

I know Droupadi didi ever since her political career in the party started in 1997. We had walked thousands of kilometers in the remote location of Mayurbhanj, Odisha to connect with people. It was our promise that we would reach every constituent in their needs. That is why she never missed any invitation and was always available to be amongst her people. This made her immensely popular and she emerged as an invincible leader paving her way to people's hearts quietly. She would always be well-mannered and never lose her temper even in the toughest time. She is very spiritual, and the Local Area Development funds would always be utilized in constructing places of worship and education etc.

SANJIB MOHANTY (TAPA)

Odisha State Executive Committee Member, Bharatiya Janata Party, Bisoi, Mayurbhanj

Droupadi Murmu has traversed the path from a homemaker to become extraordinary in life. She has led a disciplined life amidst her sweet and sour family times. This discipline started from the principles of Integral education by Sri Aurobindo and gradually she was introduced to many noble paths which she embraced with open arms shaping her personality so beautifully to be worthy for the position of the President of the biggest democracy of the earth. Knowing and working with her in close quarters along with many of our party friends who helped her in politics and service for decades gives me immense joy. Her elevation to the highest post of the country, being a tribal lady, made many a speculation wrong. Maybe destiny had stored tough times to bring out the gold in her. When I look back, I realize that, being in a national party and the sequence of events look so perfect now that she adorned the top post.

NABA CHARAN MAJHI

Member of Legislative Assembly, Rairangpur

I fought elections in 1990 and in 1995 for Rairangpur Assembly Constituency as an independent and Jharkhand Mukti Morcha candidate respectively. I had lost both times by a narrow margin from veteran leaders. When Droupadi didi became Vice-Chairman in 1997, she visited my home. She advised me to work with her in a national party. Since 1998, I have been working with her and campaigned for her in all the segments, be it Assembly and Parliament elections that she contested after that. I was one of her party confidants with whom she reposed a lot of faith in these four elections from 2000 to 2014. We were instrumental in shaping her political victory and strengthening the party in the district. We have a good deal of camaraderie among our party proteges and we live like a family. This bonding resulted in the rise of the party in the constituency ensuring better public service delivery. My political profile also took a good shape gradually. I won as a Member of Legislative Assembly from Rairangpur Constituency in 2019 and I am serving the five-year period now.

MANOJ KUMAR DAS (BAPI)

General Secretary of Bharatiya Janata Party in Mayurbhanj District

In 1992 urban local election, ward no.1 of Rairangpur NAC was reserved for women after the promulgation of 74th Constitutional amendment mandating the one-third reservation of women in urban local bodies. During that time, Rabi bhai and I had gone to Droupadi Didi's place to suggest her to contest the urban election on a BJP ticket. She refused our request and contested council election as independent candidate from the same word. After the maiden election defeat, she concentrated on the teaching. In the year 1997, once again, Rabi bhai invited her to his residence where we all were present and expressed his interest to field Droupadi didi as the candidate from Ward No.2 which was also reserved for woman that year. She agreed this time to join the national party and won as a Councillor from the BJP and also became the Vice-chairperson. The rest is history as they say. My biological and political family were so close as we worked hand in hand for the next two and half decades which brought immense glory to her political career. Many developmental works was done in the constituency by her passion, dedication, and hard work.

SHIV KUMAR AGRAWAL

Member, Core Committee, Pashchim Mayurbhanj Bharatiya Janata Party

I have been associated with Droupadi Didi ever since her political career began in 1997. I had a second-hand scooter which was used extensively by me and her as the pillion rider during her three-year stint as the Vice-chairperson of Rairangpur NAC. She traveled extensively across the length and breadth of Rairangpur town to maintain the cleanliness. This dedication in her won the hearts of the constituents and she was offered the party ticket to contest the Assembly election. She continued to be an MLA for two consecutive terms from 2000 to 2009 under the coalition Government of BJD and BJP. She was a Minister in her first term as well. When Droupadi didi received Pandit Nilakantha Samman for the best legislator in the year 2005, I was fortunate to accompany her to the ceremony. She had immense faith in me and would entrust me important political and personal work. I am overwhelmingly joyful to be as her team.

RASANANDA LENKA

Eminent Lawyer, Rairangpur

Droupadi did not opt for politics. But Politics opted for her. She resigned from the Government job to take better care of her children. While at Rairangpur, she decided to be an honorary teacher as the very name of Sri Aurobindo attracted her. She had to walk more than two kilometers to reach the school every morning for three years. She was punctual and loved students. The students also reciprocated for her good humour and narration of interesting stories in the class. She won goodwill because of her polite behaviour in the township, paving her way to urban local governance. She became the Councillor and the Vice-Chairman in Rairangpur NAC. Three years later, she was elected to the Assembly and was made a minister of state. She is devoid of any ego and resolved many long pending governance challenges as a minister. Despite the devastation in personal life, she maintained her best composure as the Governor of Jharkhand. Yogic practices were her best companion. Once in Raj Bhawan of Ranchi, she received 70 probationers of Odisha Judicial Service and made the visit memorable for them with her warmth and care. She would take interest in solving many problems of Rairangpur sub-division while she was the Governor of Jharkhand as well. She was kind enough to donate a fair amount of Law Journals for the enrichment of the library of Rairangpur Bar Association. The philanthropist in her blossomed with the she established a school in the native village Pahadpur imparting free high school education. She represents millions of women in the country. Her efficiency, character, honesty and sincerity made her the spontaneous choice of the public representatives in the Presidential election. She did not like publicity. She believes that her life will be glorified and gratified if her life is dedicated for the service of the country men. Let it be so.

DUSMANTA BASA

Actor, Writer, Director
Secretary, Bamanghaty Chhau Nrutya Pratisthan, Rairangpur (1998-continuing)

I know Droupadi Madam since she was working at Sri Aurobindo Integral Education: Research Centre, Rairangpur. She would discuss with me pertaining to the participation of students in Sub-Divisional Republic Day and Independent Day Celebrations in Rairangpur. In 1994, my wife Minati Basa was also a Head Master in Adarsh Gigili Bai school, ward no.:6, Rairangpur NAC. Our family bonding grew over a period of time. I was doing network marketing with her husband Shyam Charan Murmu for some time. She helped us many times when we needed it. I have done numerous Chhau Programme under her patronage for the last three decades. She is a great admirer, preserver, and promoter of Chhau. She was instrumental in the construction of 'Chhau Bhawan' in Rairangpur and aspired for its national and international recognition. I had the privilege to host her at Rairangpur Bar Association twice. She donated books worth INR 2 Lakhs and contributed from MLALAD for the construction of its Library building as well. When her heart remains in Mayubhanj, her vision encompasses the whole nation. She was a popular leader and attended the family functions of each of her constituents to the best of her ability.

SATISH CHANDRA PRATIHARI

Vice President, SLS Trust Board; Honorary Manager, SLS Memorial Residential School, Pahadpur

I have been associated with Shyam Babu and Droupadi Didi since 1997. I am a resident of Badampahar, Shyam Babu's native village. He was a good soccer player and the first person from Pahadpur village to pass the Bachelor's degree. Since Badampahar and Pahadpur are adjacent villages, we would meet often, and I organized many programmes for them. Now I am working with Mahamahim Droupadi Murmu for a social cause to impart free education. She is very passionate about the school and enquires about the same regularly amidst her busy schedules.

MAYANK MADAAN

President, Alumni Association, Sri Sri University, Cuttack

It was in 2018 that I visited Raj Bhawan Ranchi during Droupadi Madam's tenure as the Governor of Jharkhand. After the completion of her term, she stayed in her Rairangpur residence, and I was fortunate enough to seek her blessings there as well in January 2022 on the occasion of Makar Sankranti. I couldn't imagine a former Governor serving me freshly made hot and savoury "Arisa pitha" (A traditional sweet made of jaggery and rice in Odisha) herself. On 28 August 2022, when I met Madam in Rastrapati Bhawan, she was kind enough to recollect my name and the meeting was so warm as always. Now I realize that humility is the strength of a great leader who is adored by the masses.

SAROJ NALINI PARIDA

Batchmate of Droupadi Tudu, Former Student Union President for two terms: 1977-78 & 1978-79, Rama Devi Women's College, Bhubaneswar; Retired officer from Odisha Cooperative Service

Drouapdi and I were in the same batch during our college days. However, I did not interact with her much after completion of our BA in 1979. While in college, she was staying in the Adivasi Women's hostel (now known as Indira Gandhi Post-Matric Adivasi Women's Hostel or IGST). I was a day-scholar residing in Unit - 9 flat just behind the college and adjacent to her hostel. Most of the girls in the hostel had voted for me during the student union election and I was elected as the President of the college union for two consecutive terms. Prof. Rama Sundari Devi was our adviser to the student union who became the principal of the college in later years. We had invited Pradipta Kishore Das, Minister of Education, Government of Odisha as the chief guest in the Annual day programme organised by us. Brajeswari Mishra was the superintendent of the hostel where Droupadi was staying and Prof. Kanaka Manjari Mishra was teaching Economics among many others. Years later, in 2008, I met Droupadi in the Ekadasaha

(11th day observance of the demise) of Dayanidhi Singh, my friend Dr. Pravati Singh's father in Kadamchhanda village, Garadpur in Patkura constituency of Odisha. She recognised me immediately and we reminisced about our student days. She was serving her second term as an MLA then. Dayanidhi Singh was station master and station superintendent in Rairangpur and Gorumahisani respectively. Her brother Dillip Kumar Singh was one of the founding members of the Bharatiya Janata Party in Rairangpur and worked closely with Droupadi for years. Hence, many political leaders of Mayurbhanj including Droupadi had attended the ceremony. Back to Bhubaneswar from Patkura, we traveled together in the same car. I was touched by her simplicity and warmth. I feel proud to be her friend.

DHANI MARANDI

Cousin

I have been staying with my cousin Droupadi didi since I was in the sixth standard. My father is the youngest of four siblings. Singo Hatam (aunt) was the eldest and there were two more aunts. I was studying in the same class as Sipun, my nephew, but in a different school. I was studying in Kanyshram School (now Government SSD Girls High School) in Mahuldiha. I was there through the good and the bad times of the family for more than two decades.

GANESH HEMBRAM

Son-in-law, International Rugby Player

My mother-in-law used to address me Jawaen as addressed to a son-in-law in our community. Now she addresses me as a son. She is a very caring and loving mother. I love Sports and play International sports in Rugby and am a Physical Education teacher in the Government school of Odisha.

KALPANA MOHANTY

Former Colleague, Aurobindo Integral School, Rairangpur

Droupadi Didi and I would walk every day to school together. She would come from her Baidaposi (ward No. 2) home to Guru Gomke Pandit Raghunath Murmu Chhak (Square).

We would go via Sri Sathya Sai temple of ward no.3 by paying obeisance to the divine lotus feet of Swami. Itishree, her youngest daughter, would accompany us. She is a great soul with no animosity towards anyone ever. I have taught music to the students in her SLS Memorial school in Pahadpur as well. She always remembers me, and we would meet often even after she became a Minister and a Governor. I feel very close to her even after she has become the President of India.

SHASHANK KUMAR

District IT Coordinator, Bharatiya Janata Party, Mayurbhanj

Droupadi Madam was known to my mother since 2004. Subsequently, I worked in the party under her supervision. Often, she would call me her son and I found a mother in her. During the Swearing-in ceremony of the President of India, many senior leaders of the town had gone to attend the same in New Delhi. I stayed back in Rairangpur to organise a number of events viz., quiz competitions, cultural performances, hospitality of media personnel, distribution of sweets and a host of other programmes in the town to commemorate the historic occasion.

Droupadi Madam becoming the President of India gave us humongous joy worth treasuring for lifetime.

REBATI NANDA

Neighbour in Uparbeda Majhi Sahi

My three brothers and I were raised by the Tudu family. Droupadi's mother Singo was a goodlooking lady with a golden heart. My father passed away when I was 12 years old and my three brothers were younger than me. I cannot recollect the face of my father as our poor household did not even have a photograph of him. We were daily wagers and have seen abject poverty. We worked for 12 hours to earn one shera (approximately one kilogram) of rice.

My surname was 'Giri', and my grandmother Malati loved Droupadi Nani very much.

After marriage, I have taken my husband's surname 'Nanda'. My brothers have given me a space here, so I continue to stay here with my husband and two sons on my parental property.

Droupadi Nani speaks to me very lovingly every time I meet her even after being the Governor of Jharkhand. Her younger son, Nina (Sipun) would come to my house with sweets from Rairnagpur and eat rice, Bilati poda (a dish prepared by burning tomatoes), Sukua (dried fish), and whatever was prepared on that day. Sipun's demise was a shock for all of us. Droupadi nani (sister) and her children do not fuss about anything. They mingle with villagers and eat whatever is served to them. All the development work you have seen in the village could be possible due to her in this remote village.

DULARI TUDU

(Wife of Nephew Dularam Tudu), Ancestral Home, Uparbeda

My marriage was solemnized on 9 July 2011. We have twelve types of marriages in the Santhal Community. Mine was Haram Bariyat. My family received cattle, and clothes as Pana (Bride's money) from my husband's family. Droupadi Aunty, Shyam uncle, and their children Sipun and Itishree had attended my marriage in the ancestral home of Uparbeda village. Our marriage ceremony spans over 3-4 days. They would stay the whole day with us.

She would come to Makar Sankranti, Deepavali, Dasahara, and other festivals to celebrate with us. She comes regularly even now. I visited Raj Bhawan, Ranchi many times. I stood for the

Sarpanch election in 2022 but was defeated. I have an interest in serving and have some political aspirations as well. Let us see if I can serve the community like her. As per our tradition, we have kept the names of my children after her grandparents Chuda Sakra Tudu and Bhagat Shyam Tudu.

KANAKA LATA MANDAL

School friend

My father, Jugal Kishore Mandal was also a teacher at Uparbeda U.P.School and he taught both of us. She would ask her doubts after class hours, and we would study in school under the light of a lantern in the evening. She would cross the rivulet to go to Uparbeda M.E. School every day. I studied with her from class one to class seven. She was an obedient girl and would return home after her studies were complete as those were her mother's instructions which she followed diligently. Her mother loved me a lot too and we lived in a time when people cared for one another. I live with my family in Rourkela, Odisha, and feel nostalgic about our olden days now.

SANJUKTA MAJHI

Cousin, daughter of Former Minister Kartik Chandra Majhi

Droupadi didi was very good in academics and sports. My father had helped her admission to Unit 2 Girls' High School, Bhubaneswar. I am 4-5 years younger than her. I finished my education and got married in the year 1985 at an age of 23 years. She got married in 1980. We would meet sometime at family functions. We had been to Raj Bhawan, Ranchi when she was the Governor. We have gone to Rashtrapati Bhawan as well.

We were one of the 42 people from her family and friends who got an opportunity to witness the swearing-in ceremony in Central Hall of Parliament on 25 July 2022.

INDIRA OTTA

Former Colleague, Aurobindo Integral School, Rairangpur

The time during Aurobindo Integral school was all about discipline and introspection. Droupadi didi would take part in the discussion of knowledge on Sri Aurobindo's integral education and character building. She has no anger, aversion, or cravings for anything. Shewould take part in all the activities that happened in school viz., teaching, participating in the Independence Day parade, picnics, music, debate competitions, observing Shrima's Agaman Divas, and Siddhi Divas, singing devotional songs. She is an extremely industrious person and would not sit idle for even a moment. During her leisure time, she would spend time with students telling them stories of great personalities to be inspired by their teachings and life.After she joined politics, we used to meet often. Once, almost a decade ago, I went to her home and her daughter-in-law offered me tea and we spoke for a long time. She would always give me a patient hearing even if she became very busy subsequently.